Beyond the
Mission Statement

MARKETING BOOKS FROM PMP

The Kids Market: *Myths & Realities*

Marketing to American Latinos, Part I

Marketing to American Latinos, Part II

The Whole Enchilada

Beyond Bogedas: *Developing a Retail Relationship
with Hispanic Customers*

The Mirrored Window: *Focus Groups
from a Moderator's Point of View*

The Great Tween Buying Machine

Marketing Insights to Help Your Business Grow

Why People Buy Things They Don't Need

A Knight's Code of Business: *How to Achieve
Character and Competence in the Corporate World*

India Business: *Finding Opportunities
in this Big Emerging Market*

Moderating to the Max! *A Full-tilt Guide to Creative
Focus Groups and Insightful Depth Interviews*

Marketing to Leading-Edge Baby Boomers

Clear Eye for Branding: *Straight Talk on
Today's Most Powerful Business Concept*

Advertising to Baby Boomers

What's Black About It? : *Insights to Increase Your Share of
a Changing African-American Market*

Marketing to the New Super Consumer: Mom & Kid

Hispanic Marketing Grows Up:
Exploring Perceptions and Facing Realities

Religion in a Free Market: *Religious and Non-Religious Americans—
Who, What, Why, and Where*

Beyond the
Mission
Statement

Why Cause-Based Communications
Leads to True Success

JIM ARMSTRONG

PMP

PARAMOUNT MARKET PUBLISHING, INC.

Paramount Market Publishing, Inc.
301 S. Geneva Street, Suite 109
Ithaca, NY 14850
www.paramountbooks.com
Telephone: 607-275-8100; 888-787-8100 Facsimile: 607-275-8101

Publisher: James Madden
Editorial Director: Doris Walsh

This publication is designed to provide accurate and
authoritative information in regard to the subject matter covered.
It is sold with
the understanding that the publisher is not engaged in rendering
legal, accounting, or other professional services. If legal advice or
other expert assistance is required, the services of a competent
professional should be sought.

Contents

Acknowledgments

AN ENORMOUS thank you to the following businesses and organizations for helping "write" this book:

Alliance Healthcare Cooperative ▪ Art Growth Summit ▪ Arts Wisconsin ▪ The Biodiversity Project ▪ British Telecom ▪ Clif Bar ▪ City of Madison Community Services ▪ Clean Wisconsin ▪ Colorado Children's Campaign ▪ Cornell University ▪ Madison Area Municipal Storm Water Partnership ▪ Elect Women ▪ Greater Madison Convention and Visitor's Bureau ▪ Health Care Education and Training ▪ Hillary Institute ▪ Home Savings Bank ▪ IMS ▪ KaBOOM! ▪ Madison Concourse Hotel ▪ Madison Metropolitan School District ▪ Madison Schools & Community Recreation ▪ Meriter Hospital ▪ MetaStar ▪ MGE ▪ Milestones Project ▪ Next Generation Consulting ▪ Nicole Foundation ▪ PIC Wisconsin ▪ Sarvodaya USA ▪ Seer Analytics ▪ SERRV International ▪ Smith & Gesteland ▪ State Environmental Leadership Program ▪ Sustainable Woods Cooperative ▪ 211 ▪ T. Wall Properties ▪ United Way ▪ University of Wisconsin School of Veterinary Medicine ▪ Visiting Nurse Services ▪ Waukesha County Economic Development Corporation ▪ Western Resource Advocates ▪ Wingra School ▪ Wisconsin Academy of Science, Arts and Letters ▪ Wisconsin Alumni Research Foundation ▪ Wisconsin Patient Safety Institute.

Also, an enormous thank you to:

The Good For Business team for truly believing.

To Kathy, my partner in life, and truly why this book exists.

To Michael, Megan, and Emily—true causes of inspiration.

Truth is, what's good for you
is good for us and that's
good for business.

—J.A.

Preface

FINALLY, an honest approach to communications that transcends today's branding babble. Rather than the tired, worn-out outside-in approach to branding, positioning, and marketing communications, the Good For Business approach, captured here in *Beyond the Mission Statement*, speaks from the heart through a thorough understanding of the soul of an organization and its ultimate reason for being. It's an inside-out approach that's long overdue in the world of "brandiose" marketing and communications.

You won't find trite jargon, catch phrases, or simple catch-all one-liners here, only honest-to-goodness ways to authentically differentiate an organization through soul-searching and honesty. It's a refreshing approach to marketing that works. Speaking the *truth*. How novel!

The beauty of the approach is its simplicity. By answering only 10 basic, but thought-provoking questions about your organization with *honest* answers, you can position your firm, product, even yourself in a marketplace that's cluttered with irrelevant, transient and often misleading and deceptive messages and images.

And the process is inclusive, bringing together all facets of an organization to agreement as to their CAUSE, or why they exist. Skeptical? So was I! After over 25 years of doing marketing research for some of the largest and most successful firms in the U.S., I met Jim Armstrong and have worked with Good For Business on numerous projects. Although still a firm believer in marketing research, I now see it as only a tool to link the internal organization with the external environment so that the firm can begin living up to it's true CAUSE or purpose and develop effective strategies for communicating their reason for being. I now understand that *real* branding begins from taking a hard look within, not from without.

If this book doesn't help you see yourself and your organization in a truly different light, one from a viewpoint of TRUTH and honesty, you've been looking outside-in for way too long. It's time to get back to your roots and answer the question, "Why do we exist?" The answer may not only surprise you, but change both your organization and the world!

—CHARLEEN M. HEIDT

President, Research and Design

May 2006

ONE
Why Did You Get Up This Morning?

THIS BOOK CARRIES a universal truth that no business or person can deny. Just like people, businesses engage markets most successfully when they act from a place of purpose, or a place that I call *cause*.

A business or organization's cause is not only the blueprint for telling its story to all its audiences, but it also serves as a compass for overall business navigation. Businesses and organizations with a thousand or more employees and global operations use this approach. Start-ups with a single visionary entrepreneur and non-profits squeezing the most out of a budget also find value in this cause-based blueprint.

You may be thinking, "I don't have time for this; get me the latest business book about swimming with sharks, searching for cheese, or the unadulterated joys of downsizing." This is a forgivable reaction, but you do have time for this and if you don't think you do, you should make time, because this book is about the kind of businesses that are created to stand the test of time. It can help you steer clear of trendy traps of cool strategy and foolproof case studies crying out to be imitated. It is filled with both common sense affirmations and visionary declarations. It comes from a place where purpose and passion intersect and principle and profit aim to work in harmony. It comes from a place that believes "*A business isn't a brand to be built, but a cause to be believed in.*"®

In the purest business sense, "cause" is the true, authentic, genuine reason your business or organization exists. Your cause begins to reveal itself when you and your employees ask, "Why do we do what we do?" *Why* is the most important question when developing communications for an organization or a business. When you answer *Why?* you begin to capture your business purpose or cause. *Cause* is where your business's passion lives. This is where your organization's truth resides. When you begin to integrate your real passion and truth into your communications, or for that matter, any strategic endeavor, good things are bound to happen.

So ask yourself:

- Why does a CEO get up in the morning (or work through the night) to produce or provide something?

- Why does an employee devote his or her waking moments (and often dreams—but hopefully not nightmares) to a particular business or organization?

- Out of all the jobs in the world, why have you chosen what you do?

- Out of all the products and services in the world, why have you decided that making this or selling that is the one you are committing to?

When you ask why, the undeniable reason for a business's existence emerges in all its energetic glory or confident dignity and force. When you truly answer why, you go beyond the superficiality of believing you "exist to make a profit" or the detached and subservient purpose of "my company exists to increase shareholder wealth." You find yourself and your business propelled to a bountiful region where business as usual is the death knell. This is a territory abundant with real meaning, inspiration, and the opportunity for success.

This is the place where your passion flows into all your communications. It affects how you speak with the marketplace, how you connect internally with your employees, how your leadership team communicates, and how you carry on an ongoing and inspiring dialogue within yourself. Your cause becomes the foundation for creating messages that are honest, hype-free, void of spin, manipulation, and "brandiose" marketing. Asking *Why?* is a galvanizing means to build a strong, enduring bridge over the *brand canyon*.

Rant and Realization

Personally, this book serves as my affirmation on what business is meant to be. When I was a radical college student, I thought business was the dark side. Anarchy was a better option than capitalism. Punctuate this with the fact that I went to graduate school and got a degree in poetry (turning away from a law school opportunity), and you get a feel for where I got this idealistic, yet unrealistic and unfair appraisal of business. Unfortunately, this appraisal appeared to be validated when, Masters Degree in Poetry in one hand and no job in another, I applied and got a "real job" as a copywriter. I loved the creative aspects of the job, but was completely disillusioned when I witnessed the inhuman interactions of the workplace and the value systems that triggered those interactions. It appeared to be a highly dysfunctional dynamic.

Having been cloistered in academia, teaching, and jobs in social work, I hadn't yet had a juicy taste of business (or "unconscious commerce" as I then liked to call it). But boy, did this experience serve up a gluttonous plate of unsavory images and unhealthy workplace relationships. I saw burned-out senior account executives showing up at the urinal at 8 a.m. with a beer in hand. Secretaries were scolded for not putting enough honey in a boss's tea. Junior account executives wore icons on their wristwatches reminding them to pray. Fear flowed out of the markers of art directors. No women were in the boardrooms. Not too many courageous men were there either.

This was a world where the guys and gals each knew their place. A world where the trappings of power were played out in ways that caught the most good-hearted and well-intentioned and released them back into their cubicles and departments with a new and "real" set of operational ethics that put items like balance, respect, integrity, transparency, truth, and family on the soft or weak side of the ledger. I asked myself, "Is this the way of business?" More importantly, I asked, "If this *is* the way of business, *why* does it need to be this way?"

Brand Canyon

What is the plural of abyss? I'd like to know because many of them— small and shallow and large and infinite—sculpted yesterday's, and continue to shape today's, brandscape. It's an abyss most often carved out when core ethics, be they personal or professional, clash with market promise.

Case in point: I was once working on a branded cereal account that was just one of many pledging allegiance to the multi-multi corporation. The branding team from the client side was instructed by the multi-multi to reposition what was an established adult cereal as a kid's cereal. This cereal tasted, smelled, and looked grown-up. It had no child-like qualities. Kids were going to turn their noses at even the sight of a bowl of this stuff. Yet, the strategy was to simply change the packaging from an adult look to one that had a kid's look and couple the box's cosmetic makeover with some Saturday morning–break commercials.

Saturday morning TV is a commercial chasm in itself, but combine it with the values packaged within the client's marketing team, and the gulf of greed widens to near apocalyptic proportions. There were ten members of the client cereal team. All ten were men. Eight had no children, primarily because they didn't like kids. The two that did have kids worked around-the-clock, hoping to avoid the pitfalls of parenting.

I had experienced these gaps before and swallowed their emptiness into a widening disbelief system. Evidently, this was the breaking point. When I realized that there was no connection between the values, beliefs, and principles of the branding team and the promise they were making to the marketplace, I also realized that a fundamental shift had to occur. This shift had to result not just in bridging the gap between personal and professional values and the value proposition made to the customer and other stakeholders, but it had to actually close and eliminate the gap. From that point on, there was no room in my life for the brand canyon.

This Is Not Cause-related Marketing

My company, Good For Business, begins conversations with businesses and organizations by asking *Why?* and when the honest-to-goodness answer to that question emerges, it takes the form of the *cause*. This *cause* becomes the heartbeat of communications as well as the driver of actual business strategy.

But this *cause* must not be confused with cause-related marketing. Cause-related marketing is a tactical tool employed to build strategic bridges between key stakeholder groups. It's a tactic that usually has two key consenting parties: One is typically a business, the other is a non-profit or non-governmental organization (NGO) with a social or environmental issue. Together they form a mutually rewarding alliance. The alliance can be formed to raise awareness, raise funds in support of an organization, or raise positive perceptions about both members of the alliance. Sometimes there are links between the missions and values of the business and non-profit or the products and services of the business and the non-profit. Often there is no linkage. The relationship could be based on the personal concerns and interests of a CEO or other influential business.

I'll be so bold as to say that if a business does all the hard work necessary to unearth and validate its cause, that cause in and of itself, if pursued and achieved, will create a positive social or environmental impact. There is no need for the business to partner with a non-profit in order to create social or environmental good. The managers realize that the business's purpose, behavior, and interactions with all of its stakeholders are an engine for positive outcome.

This is not to say that a business, once it understands its cause should not partner with and support social and environmental issues. These kinds of partnerships become tactics relevant to enhancing and emboldening the company cause. The cause will also result in more effective marketing endeavors that are void of greenwashing, white-washing, and marriages of convenience. Imagine the impact of a business that knows, understands, and embraces its cause and then partners with a non-profit that is passionately engaging in a social or environmental issue that is a true reflection of that corporate cause.

This Is Not Corporate Social Responsibility

The genesis for Good For Business emerged during the embryonic stage of the Corporate Social Responsibility (CSR) movement in the United States. Some say it is still and always will be embryonic. I disagree! My initial approach was forged and fortified with all the necessary ingredients of social responsibility: transparency, integrity, mutual respect and understanding, sustainability, authenticity, and so on. I also have to confess I relied on the language of CSR, the data and research supporting it, the case studies, and the placing of the pioneers on inspiring pedestals to make the case. I championed the movement with gusto and guts. Not many thought at the time I could make a living doing business this way. However, it wasn't long after the birth of Good For Business that I began to realize the business had its own universal, innovative, socially responsible language and behavior. I found Good For Business blending local words and actions with the global language and best practices flowing through with the CSR wave. As clients were engaged with the business-as-a-cause philosophy, which we also refer to as "Mission in a Message," they too began to reveal their own story of responsibility.

The stories that appear in the following chapters are those of some of our clients. I didn't put CSR lingo or consultant-speak into our clients' mouths. Their stories were constructed via their hearts and minds and the "soul" of the business or organization. They reveal a collective responsibility to the local and global communities in which they do business.

These stories reflect a realization that a business can make a profit as it fulfills the responsibility of an honorable citizen concerned about more than the bottom line. Peter Drucker realized this half a century ago in *The Practice of Management*: "If we want to know what a business is, we have to start with its purpose. And its purpose must lie outside of the business itself. In fact, it must lie in society since a business enterprise is an organ of society." Drucker goes on to say, "Profit is not the explanation or rationale of business behavior and business decisions, but the test of their validity."

David Batstone, Professor of Ethics and formerly the National Endowment for the Humanities Chair at the University of San Francisco, notes "Organizations of every size should have souls that can easily be discerned by the public. The soul of a company should not be the result of a creative public relations campaign; rather, it should be the collect result of the souls of every individual within the company. When senior executives create a culture that is without a strong ethical or moral foundation, the company will have no discernible soul."

To truly succeed a business must come to grips with its need to be transparent, to engage with integrity, to respect others and to communicate its unique value to the world. Through the process of coming to grips, business leaders, managers and employees naturally recognize social responsibility as an undeniable part of their business's DNA. How they express or capture it is all theirs. If they use the principles and language of CSR to do it, so be it. But if their business's character, personality and "soul" doesn't depend on the CSR dictionary for explaining itself, that is also fine.

This is not to say that Corporate Social Responsibility has no place in this cause proposition. It certainly does. But to helm an enterprise that makes its way through the world led by cause and propelled by purpose, managers don't need to complete a social audit, attend a CSR workshop, or read all there is on corporate citizenship. It is great if business leaders do this, but it's neither the litmus test nor price for entry into the world of cause.

This Is Not the Branding Book of the Month

Truth be told, it's difficult for me to give credence to the whole concept of brand. It is an ugly word. It's also a word that has been stretched, shrunk, lobotomized, transfused, worshiped, disparaged, and worst of all industrialized. It has become a consultant's crutch, a CEO's undoing or just-doing, a marketing department's gravest sin or salvation, and the public's security blanket and barometer for bull. It has become everything from a corporate religion with all kinds of marketing mantras and NASCAR decals to quietly embossed logos on baby bottles and anti-branding that becomes a brand itself. *Brand Gap, Cultural Branding, Brand Portfolio Strategy, 22 Immutable Laws of Branding, A New Brand World, The Brand You 50, Emotional Branding, Designing Brand Entity, Brand Babble* are just a few of the 7,032 titles you come up with if you go to Amazon and search under books for brand. That's a lot of brand to cover. The whole phenomenon smacks of self-help books (and there's nothing wrong with that) in that the more you read, the more you need. The need expands beyond the books to workshops, retreats, guidebooks, organizational modeling, and infusion into all kinds of other trends and movements from Total Quality Management (TQM) and Corporate Intelligence (CI) to, would you believe, Brand Downsizing.

You can count on just about every book, consultant, workshop and wiz of the week to have a different definition of brand. That's a big chunk of why there are so many problems with the brand concept. It is what you make it to be, void of any natural, authentic meaning. Brands are built, shaped, packaged, spun and when these approaches run dry, the brand gurus take us to places of "deeper meaning." But this kind of meaning often is simply a means to the same end—selling or increasing market share or crushing competition via a "killer advantage" (no, wait a minute, let's spin that to "lover advantage").

Think about it. Doesn't the word "brand" conjure up something impersonal, detached, and removed from reality? I think it does and that's why the business world tries so darn hard to make it personal, connected, and a critical part of your life. Some say branding is a school of marketing that emerged from the successes achieved by businesses that integrated consistency and truth throughout every level of communications and actions. Fine. Let it be. And let it serve, not lead, the higher purpose of business, which I call *cause*. If you walk away with anything from this book, it will be the realization that "*A business isn't a brand to be built, but a cause to be believed in.*"®

This Isn't About Your Mission Statement

Chances are you have worked long and hard on crafting a mission statement. A mission statement usually says *what* you do and perhaps *how* you do it. But seldom does a mission statement say *why* you do *what* you do. When a business's or organization's mission statement does have a *why*, it tends to be vibrant, dynamic, real and dare we say compassionate *if* the "why" transcends the making of money.

Here's a good way to tell the difference between a mission statement and the cause of your business. Right now, recite, word for word your mission statement. **Is it something you can chant or shout in the shower in the morning?** Is it something that gets you up and out of bed in the morning? Is it something that serves as your guide when you bump into it throughout your day? Mission statements often are painstakingly written with impressive words that reflect honorable thinking. They often end up being longer than they need to be and, unless coerced by a performance review, not a snap to memorize. A true cause doesn't need to be memorized; it just rolls off the tongue. This book isn't about helping you write or rewrite your mission statement. It's about helping you unearth, validate, and capture your business cause. That's cause enough to read it.

Cause vs. Mission

Here's the difference between a mission statement and a business cause:

The Mission: Our mission is to provide a vibrant, caring, and safe learning community that enhances and empowers the lives of young people by offering optimal opportunities for intellectual, emotional, physical, and aesthetic growth.

The Cause: *To make learning joyful*

The Mission: To support scientific research at the university by moving inventions arising from university research to the marketplace, for the benefit of the university, the inventor and society as a whole and investing licensing proceeds to fund further research at the university.

The Cause: *Ensure our discoveries improve the human condition.*

The Mission: To listen, learn from, and encourage collaborative dialogue among businesses and regional resources—who then mobilize initiatives addressing issues that hamper economic prosperity, growth and business retention.

The Cause: *Creating courageous business conversation*

The Mission: To create and disseminate knowledge about hospitality management. We achieve this through: Teaching; the faculty disseminates knowledge through outstanding and rigorous instruction and other activities that lead to learning with an industry focus. We create a learning and educational environment that nurtures critical thinking, intellectual growth, and taking personal responsibility. Research; the faculty creates knowledge that influences the industry and the academic community. We engage in disciplined, industry-focused research, and other intellectual contributions that ultimately will affect industry practice. Industry relations and service; the faculty both serves the industry, students, alumni, the School, university, academia, and community and cultivates relationships with industry professionals and companies.

The Cause: *Creating a global community of hospitality leaders who change the world*

What This Book Will Do and Why

This book will reveal the power of seeing your business as a cause by sharing with you stories of other businesses and organizations who operate from a place of cause. It will help you understand the process our clients go through as they find and champion their cause and provide examples of how they have teased out the answers to ten questions and then applied them to materials for marketing communication. These communication plans serve as blueprints for cause-based communications. They can help you create your own document that will be of immense value in both short and long-term strategic planning. Once your business realizes its true purpose and converts that purpose into a livable, tangible principle, it becomes a beacon not only for telling your story, but also the benchmark for making key business decisions. If a new product or service aligns with or clashes with your cause, that will tell you a lot about what is the right decision. You will be able to easily assess whether your modes of operation or your supply chain reflect and are inspired by your cause, or if they dilute or compromise your cause. You will see why this process and the roadmap it produces are of immense value when driving your business to where it can thrive, prosper, and increasingly benefit all of your crucial communities: employees, customers, suppliers, and the place you live and work. You will find how to find and define the cause you can sing in the shower.

Although some of the resulting communications appear in these pages in black and white, you are also invited to visit our website, *www.goodforbusiness.com/book*. There you will see actual examples of the communications created based on the Mission-in-a-Message strategies.

Verses which do not teach us new and moving truths do not deserve to be read.

                                                    Voltaire

TWO
Why Does Your Business Do What It Does?

WHEN DEVELOPING cause-based communications, this is the first question asked, and it sets the stage for everything else. If you are committed to answering this question truthfully and with authenticity and courage, your answer will lead to crystal-clear answers to all the other questions in your brief. Typically, this question, "Why does your business do what it does? consumes about 40 to 50 percent of the time dedicated to creating the communications strategy. But when this first question is answered with passion and honesty, the answers to the remaining questions will flow. It is highly recommended—no, it is required—that those who participate in answering this question be the real leadership team of your organization.

The key to unearthing and validating your cause is always to remember that you're not talking about *what* you do. You're talking about *why* you do it. You're not crafting a mission statement, framing a vision statement or bringing forth and celebrating core values. You're asking yourself: "Why do we have the mission we have?" "Why is our vision statement our vision?" "Why have we selected these values to be our values?" The difference between simply asking *what* versus *why* is the difference between small talk and thoughtful expression that leads to real knowledge and understanding.

Picture a father and his young son walking though the zoo. The son points to a peacock and asks the father, "What is that?" The father can simply answer, "That is a peacock." But what if the son then asks, "Why does the peacock have those kinds of feathers?" Now the father faces a question where the answer probably doesn't immediately roll off the tongue. The father is either going through his memory files to see if that answer is there, or he and his son engage in a conversation of curiosity where they both may try to theorize why the bird's plumes are the way they are, or they promise to both visit the nearest encyclopedia for the answer.

Whatever the result, it is deeper than a simple "what" answer. Imagine if the son asks his father an even more provocative question like "Why does the peacock exist?" or "Why do I exist, Dad?" Take this analogy to the boardroom or retreat or coffee shop where your *why* discussion will take place. Don't settle for the superficial response to *why* you are in business. Don't settle for a "what" response. These answers can range from the classic, "We provide excellent products," to "We provide first class service," to "We exist to make a lot of money." All of these are legitimate responses to what products and services you provide and the rewards you hope for providing them. But they don't deal with *why* you want to provide excellent products or *why* you want to provide great service or *why* you want to make tons of cash.

For too long, business has scoffed at these kinds of deep conversations, calling them "soft." For too long business has called the act of making money the "hard" part. They've gotten it wrong. And we, as a society and planet, have paid dearly for it. To keep the analogies going, it's a lot like a relationship. Imagine married people who spend most of their year busy doing things—things that keep them from really getting to know what resides deep in their own hearts and in the minds of their life partners. "Busy" is used a lot in this dynamic. "We're too busy to stop and catch our breath," or "We get so busy that there's no time for us." Eventually, 20 or 30 years later (or just 2 to 3 years later depending on the relationship), they decide it's time to define themselves not necessarily by all the *what* they have done in their lives, but *why* they did those things. Call it a midlife crisis or whatever, but it happens a lot. And when it does, the outcomes can be mild or extreme.

When businesses ask the *why* question earlier rather than later, they reduce the propensity for an identity crisis. Asking *why* is a powerful way for both a person and a corporation to "know thyself," and knowing thyself is a strategic stronghold according to both ancient philosophy and current organizational and personal development doctrines.

Here are some examples of business and organizational causes we have helped our clients unearth and validate. Often the cause sounds and feels like a realization or revelation. The examples cover a range of sectors, from health care and hospitality, to the arts, environment, energy and research.

Business/Organization	Cause
health care cooperative	To create premium care at the most affordable price.
eco-literacy initiative	To preserve and protect the Great Lakes.
family planning program	To make the world a better place for women.
environmental organization	To protect clean water and clean air for today and tomorrow.
arts advocacy organization	To ensure everyone, everywhere, experiences the arts.
city government program	To improve the quality of early childhood education, hereby improving our economic security and quality of life.
global communications company	To create a better world through better communications.
convention and visitor's bureau	To make sure as many people as possible experience the fact that we meet both their emotional and intellectual needs.
business application development company	To solve business problems with technology and integrity.
hotel	To create a sense of community, internally and externally.

Business/Organization	Cause
public schools	To make sure taxpayers realize the wisdom of their investment in public education.
women's political movement	To elect more women to high public national office.
hospital	To fulfill the honor to serve.
bank	To personally help.
energy company	To be held responsible for the community and its energy.
recreational program	To enhance the quality of life for individuals by providing year-round recreation and enrichment opportunities accessible to all.
market research company	Creating better places to live and work.
cycling foundation	To make positive change in the world of cycling.
international leadership institute	Great leadership improves the human condition.
medical insurance corporation	To help eliminate fear from the practice of medicine.
Sri Lanka relief fund	To help us share ourselves for the good of all.
data analytics firm	To integrate, analyze and provide actionable intelligence for commercial and social sector success.
national environmental group	To protect the nation's environment by making state activist groups successful.
CPA firm	To create financially successful, caring and dynamic relationships that result in more than balancing the books.
sustainable woods cooperative	To raise awareness of the benefits of sustainable forest products and increase demand for them.
municiple storm water partnership	To improve the quality and reduce the quantity of urban runoff.
call for help social service	To improve the public's accessibility to vital health and human services, resulting in more effective solutions.

Business/Organization	Cause
national non-profit	To improve the well-being of all children and their communities through play.
social services agency	To build a stronger community for all by strengthening health and human services and eliminating root causes of problems.
vet school	To advance animal and human health with compassion and science.
visiting nurse service	To ensure the choice for home care is a worthy choice.
records & storage company	Positive impact.
academy of science, arts & letters	To connect people and ideas to create a better state.
economic development corporation	To create the context for courageous business conversations.
western environmental advocacy group	To preserve and protect the environment of the interior West.
private school	To create a school where children find joy in learning.
patient safety institute	To make our community the safest place for health care.
international fair trader	To alleviate poverty.
healthcare quality improvement organization	To ensure the healthiest lives possible.
property development company	To create places where people interact.
university research foundation	To ensure our discoveries improve the human condition.
masters in hospitality program	To create a global community of hospitality leaders who change the world.
statewide child advocacy group	To relentlessly provide hope and opportunity for every child in the state.
global photography project	To heal divisiveness through individual action.

Chances are your reaction to these "causes" is something like this: "Well, that makes sense," or "Well, who wouldn't want that?" or "That's a universal truth," or "How idealistic can that business be?" If these are your reactions, they are legitimate, logical, and pushing you into the business-as-a-cause dynamic.

You see that none of these causes are really about making a truckload of money although these businesses and organizations are some of the most lucrative around. You will also notice, that although driven by ideals, most of these causes are void of a corporate or organizational ego. In either direct or subtle ways, they all are about serving a greater good. And when any business or for that matter any individual or group of individuals realizes that serving the greater good is the real reason for commercial existence, powerful forces come into play. These forces range from reduced turnover and increased loyalty among employees, to willingness of customers to pay a bit more for your product or service, to communities that are eager for you to do business on their main streets. There is a ton of data out there supporting these results. The point is that you can get all the data, do all the analysis, commission the strategic exploration, research, validate and then determine that it **does** make sense to run a business based on a core purpose because that core purpose **can** be profitable. But you don't need to. In fact, that process could very well suck the life out of your purpose and make it so calculated, methodical, and sanitized that it loses the very caché that makes it compelling.

You need to go for it because it is the right thing to do and our stay here on earth is far too short to do things we know in our heart of hearts are the wrong things to do. It's called positive common sense, and who ever said we have too much of that? Not that we won't make mistakes and have our failures. That's not what is meant here by the "wrong" thing. You can move forward, make mistakes, sacrifice, and stumble, but also experience glorious successes and market triumphs based on an uncompromising drive to do the right thing. What could be better than succeeding at something and doing it with an unwavering commitment to something that will make life better for others and yourself?

Searching the Soul

Although these causes may at first seem very straightforward and obvious, their simplicity and clarity is the result of intense soul and strategic searching. As mentioned earlier, for far too long, this view has been called the "soft" side of business. That is probably because those in business really knew it was the "hard" stuff and didn't have the courage to face it and deal with it.

It's a lot like love. Those individuals who can love and be loved seem to be a lot stronger and happier than those who can't. Imagine your business being loved by all your stakeholders and your business being able to love them. Who would have thought they would be the key business indicators? So let's put all this love stuff in context. The purpose of this book is to reveal the power of communicating your cause. Which means letting your stakeholders know you love them. If this is all totally new to you, you can use "appreciate" and "respect" instead of love. But if you are completely with me at this point, go ahead and get passionate and embrace the realization that you and your company or organization are here to serve. This just isn't a matter of getting the gumption to say, "I love you." Your words require actions. Those actions must drip with passion, truth, and authenticity. In return, you'll have employees, customers and share-holders happy they have finally found a business or product or ser-vice that really cares about them and compels them to care about you. It's a relationship that can stand the test of time, trends, hype, spin and buzz.

With that digression, let's move forward with some "cause stud-ies." These studies reflect actual clients who have gone through the

Mission-in-a-Message process and, from all appearances, have come out the better for it. All cause studies begin with review of how they answered Question One. I have selected case studies from diverse business and social arenas so you can see that you can do this no matter what your specific business or non-profit sector happens to be. Several snapshot Mission-in-a-Message samples are provided for your review in Chapter Eight.

The ideals which have always shone before me and filled me with the joy of living are goodness, beauty and truth. To make a goal of comfort or happiness has never appealed to me; a system of ethics built on this basis would be sufficient only for a herd of cattle.

Albert Einstein

THREE
This Bank's Interest Is Very Personal

THANKS TO ITS 100-year commitment to community, Home Savings Bank has made sure its hometown never turned into Pottersville, that soulless town in *It's a Wonderful Life*. And it hasn't. Its hometown, Madison, Wisconsin, is consistently ranked as a top city for work, life, and play by media from *Money Magazine* and *Forbes* to *Outside* and *Ladies Home Journal*. I'm not saying the bank is solely responsible for this, but as the community's only locally owned, independent bank, the institution does reflect the values and attributes of the community. Indeed, the bank's leadership took a page out of *It's A Wonderful Life:* The current president is the son of the former president of the bank.

The president is involved in all kinds of boards and activities throughout the community—from the board of the children's museum to the chairman of a fundraising run for the university's athletic department. All the employees and associates of the bank are encouraged to be involved in the community they care so much about. For years, the bank has been involved in many initiatives intended to make the quality of life better, from support of public education to environmentally sensitive business practices. It also has offered competitive and innovative financial products to the marketplace.

However, despite its continuous community citizenship and strong services and customer offerings, it was faced with one mighty obstacle: its size. Because it is local and independent, it is often dwarfed by the marketing and communication efforts of the big boys—the mega-banks and branches. Because of this David and Goliath scenario, the story of the bank didn't get the mindshare it deserved. And, because of what can be regarded as the commoditization of banking, executives of Home Savings often felt compelled to focus their communications on the promotion of interest rates and incentives at the expense of their true purpose for being a bank. The leaders of the bank realized these unhealthy communication and marketing issues and decided to alter the brandscape and begin to make their messaging truly reflect and champion their cause. The timing was also crucial in that the bank's leaders had recently completed strategic business plans that included the development of product lines and services and an audience analysis as well as some competitive analysis.

So, what is the bank's cause? How did we unearth it? How has its cause influenced its communications?

Although I've harped about the fact that the cause of a business isn't its mission, if a business has a mission statement, it's often a good place to start the search for cause. The organization's reaction to its mission statement will tell me a lot. Does the leadership team revere it or find it a meaningless collection of words? Does the organization believe the mission statement captures what it does, or is it an inaccurate reflection of the organization? Does the statement breathe? Does it have integrity? Is it a living document? Or file fodder?

I like to dissect the mission statement. It is much like dissecting sentences in grade school by separating the action words from those words being acted upon. I like to see what kind of adjectives or adverbs are in the statement, if any. I like to study the construction, whether it is a short and sweet mission or one that twists and turns and goes on and on.

So, we began by looking at the current mission statement of the bank. By we, I mean the president of the bank, the marketing director, the COO, the CIO, the head of HR, and several leadership loan officers and board members. I put the current mission up on the easel for review and comment. The statement reads: *We help our depositors/owners achieve and celebrate important life events.*

During our opening discussion, I found that the team hadn't been referring to the mission statement on a regular basis. I surmised the reason for this neglect was because of ongoing review and understanding of key stakeholder groups, depositors, employees, and the organization itself, and what they meant to the bank. With all this strategizing going on, we discussed what would be a relevant mission statement. Guess what? The two words you can drive a convoy of trucks through popped up—*quality* and *service.* This time they were presented in the context of the bank being a "financial center dedicated to quality, personal service." This is true. But it's also true for many banks or financial institutions. And, besides the lack of distinction in this statement, what do *quality* and *service* really mean? I'm looking for specifics and deeper contexts. I'm talking about words that have become catchall crutches for business, throwing them away, and standing tall through unique strengths and attributes.

Give me another word for *quality,* or two words, or a sentence, or even a symbol or metaphor. The word *personalized* then popped up. The leaders of the bank believed they provided a kind of personalized service unfound in the marketplace. Combining this with the bank's array of innovative services revealed a new value proposition: *personalized service and choice products that help assure financial strength and independence.* Sounds good, but the people in the room were still looking for a passionate point of difference, something that not only sounded good, but also felt great. Since we were discussing what makes the bank different and why that difference is a market benefit, I asked them to share with me those attributes, common and unique, that describe the bank. Here is a summary of what I heard.

This bank has been around for over 100 years. That's a long, long time. There is a true sense of pride in that history. This is a smaller bank, so associates can have more of an impact; a bigger bank has more cogs in the gear and you can't directly make a difference. Here everyone can have an impact within the organization. This bank has an unyielding commitment to the community, more than any other institution. While other banks are focused primarily at the institutional level, generalizing needs and not looking at individual needs, this bank looks directly at individual needs and embraces the reality that members are owners. This is an independent institution, the only one in the region. It's small, sustainable, home-based. Its human scale allows people to truly know and connect with other people. Customers and co-workers become friends here. As a group we began to realize that if this bank wasn't around, the community would be commoditized and homogenized. There would be a group of bankers who weren't going home very happy at night because they had to work for an institution void of *personalization* and *community*, an institution that put profit above all else.

Home Savings Bank was allowing its associates to have a personal impact. The size of the bank was an advantage because what could take days at another bank could be done in 10 to 15 minutes here. Bigger organizations create products that are interchangeable goods. This brings incredible efficiency and lower pricing, but in order to do it, the individual is taken out of the product. It all becomes plain vanilla.

Home Savings isn't plain vanilla. Universal mortgage applications are used throughout the whole industry, whereas we can make exceptions for our customers so they feel like individuals. Some of the bigger banks are doing automated underwriting and creating credit scores that are computer generated. Loan officers become sales people instead of credit analysts. They're not complete decision makers because the computer credit score tells them the decision. That's not what happens at this bank. At larger banks, employees can start to feel like a commodity to the organization. The associates at this bank are extremely pleased to be in an environment that celebrates both the power of teamwork and the individual. In other banks an employee may have to say, "I can't help you because your credit score is 619," and the customer becomes a number. But not everyone has perfect credit. Most of the time there is an opportunity to go deeper than the credit score and create a personal relationship with the customer. There that level of human interaction thrives.

You may ask why don't all the banks behave this way? Well, they are succumbing to that portion of customer pressure that wants the best terms or rates and are willing to give up the investment in personal service in order to offer lower rates. The real power of Home Savings is that it has created an institution where there is great personal service and great rates.

Differentiating Concepts

Our work then began to shed light on some challenging and differentiating concepts. There is this idea of efficiency versus customized organizations. Efficiency here means commodity, low margin, and high volume. The people you want in this environment are not driven by creativity, but are satisfied doing things with precision. Customized means high margin and lower volume. The people here are more creative and individualistic. Up to this point, the bank's leadership team had danced around this dichotomy. None of them would be satisfied in the commodity world; they believe it is their brute (their word, not mine) determination in spite of what's happening in the industry that keeps them in business. It is in the delivery side where Home Savings brings something different to the table, where the uniqueness lies. We talked about place-based economic development and how this bank is place-based, how members, associates, and neighborhoods come together. With that sense of place there is great sense of our history here. The associates believe they are stewards for the organization. They want this organization to exist 50 years from now. For other banks, do the stockholders really care about this? Here, there is the warmth of a smaller organization. It's personal and emotional. Customers don't get lost in the process of numbers like they would at a larger organization. There isn't the power struggle that is witnessed at larger banks. There isn't the huge ego at this bank.

To assure the members' personal financial strength and well-being, they make certain decisions that help them to develop good financial skills. Part of the bank's original mission statement was to provide education to its customers. The bank's leaders believe in the adage, "we listen, we respond, you benefit," as the formula for product development. They have the best, and maybe only, junior savings program, and a checking program that helps young people learn to write checks. Other new unique products include *fear-free* checking and *green* checking.

The main struggle is marketing these products to make them profitable enough. Our communications need to explain our portfolio of products and what we do in order to have people seek us out. Customers need to realize that there's a difference and there's a value. How does the bank get people's attention and get beyond the percentage rate? How does it use intimate customer knowledge in the best interest of the customer? The bank actually puts empathy in its products, which bucks the commodity trend.

At the bank, community involvement is expected, but to have someone be *personally* delighted is motivating. The bank will and does change products based on what its associates hear because they interact face-to-face. They bring a more personal level of service, and really listen to the customer's situation, and, after listening, their first word is not "no." They see what can be worked out.

The service part we talked about at the beginning of this chapter enters when associates show options, provide the additional service, listen to the customer and find out what they need, and provide people with more than hope. Regardless of who walks in the door, they are dedicated to giving great service. Everyone is important and valuable. They work with customers wherever they start, and work with them to get to a better place. They try to offer options and actually take the time to explore the options. Other banks develop their systems to support their product; they can have artificial human touch put into it, but underneath it all, it is not real. Leaders must believe in this human touch. Here the bank president will ask, "What do your customers need? What are they asking?" The management team is progressive and forward like the state and community in which they operate. So, with all this great background and input, I suggested to the leadership team that they consider this very short and sweet cause:

Personally Help

We exist to personally help. We personally help people build financial freedom. We personally help our neighbors. We personally help one another. We personally help on all kinds of levels.

Here, a chord was struck that turned deep understanding and values into action and benefit. People need to be thinking and acting personally at all levels. This is their "face-to-face, you're not a number" cause.

The Bank's Cause and Effect

How did the bank leaders put their cause into action, particularly into their marketing messages?

They came to grips with the fact, organizationally, that they would not accomplish their mission and cause if they don't tell their story. They can't bring the customers in to have the personal relationships without communicating. They fully realized they couldn't survive in today's marketplace without communicating.

Because it is not as conveniently located as some other banks, it has to get the message out, so that potential customers understand there is additional value to banking with Home Savings. It has special people, special products, and special services. But how do bank leaders communicate the intention behind their products and services? Customers don't perceive financial products as being significantly different. Home Savings Bank doesn't have as large a budget as other banks that are plastering their great rates all over town.

If they truly are in a commodity world that competes on rate, they are not in a good situation, but if there are factors beyond rate, then it is imperative to tell their story. The outcome will depend on the values and perceptions of customers; some may care only about rate, some care about rate *plus*. There is a bit of that David and Goliath thing here—the need to compete with banks that have many, many bank branches. This bank must be on consistent message over time to reinforce its proposition, and never grow weary of it.

Meeting the Competition

This bank's competitive climate is complex. It starts of course with credit unions, large banks and brokerage and mortgage houses and concludes with the money needed to effectively advertise. In-between, there are all kinds of other obstacles. Many of the larger banks have branches. It is applying the 80/20 rule (80 percent of your customers give you 20 percent of your profits) but it needs to find out who the 20 percent of customers are and pay attention to them. It has a need to find the key to more profitable customers. It doesn't want to wind up having an appeal that makes unprofitable customers flock to it. In the banking industry, a profitable customer has a big balance, low yielding accounts, OR bounces a lot of checks but always pays the service fees for the bounced checks. An unprofitable customer is one with a lot of transactions, a $100 balance, but never bounces a check.

Another obstacle is the fact that customers don't know the bank is here. Often seen as a home loan institution, people don't perceive it as a bank. Commercially, its size is a barrier to handling larger loans.

It is not up-to-date with technology and is a late-adopter to online banking, bill pay, and ATM machines. The bank is viewed as not too convenient in terms of locations. Its website doesn't say it offers products like car loans and student loans, so people don't think of it as a full-service bank. More loan information needs to be available on the website. People don't know the bank has local decision-making and how quickly it can approve a loan. Competitors tell its customers it is stodgy and not as trendy.

But, with all that adversity, this is a bank with a great story to tell and plenty to offer its customers.

It is the region's only independent, member-owned bank. Its independence allows it to serve customers in a more personal, flexible, and innovative way. Customers have access to any of its associates' direct phone numbers, and yes, there is a live receptionist who actually answers calls. Customers bank with Home Savings associates on a first-name basis and there is seldom a need for associates to check in with corporate headquarters before they can make a decision regarding customer accounts and needs. This is the corporate headquarters! From savings accounts, checking accounts, and money market programs to business checking accounts, mortgage loans, home equity loans, and 24-hour online banking, its products have been created based on listening to its customers. And the products can be further customized based on each customer's unique needs. Its rates are often the best in the market. Add to all this the bank's total commitment to the long-term sustainability of its community. This bank's leaders and employees believe it is their responsibility to not only strengthen a customers financial well-being, but also the environmental, social, and cultural well-being of this special place they call home, and they've been doing it for over 100 years.

Looking at the strengths and weaknesses, the real value proposition, and the key benefit, the promise of the bank is that it will personally help you build your financial health and freedom. The bank's leaders determined their key word to be *personally*. The bank's key audience is a customer in the middle market, aged 35 to 55, with an income of $30,000 to $100,000. This profile makes up 47 percent of its current customer base.

Communicating the Message

This entire Mission-in-a-Message process caused the bank to step back and truly recast its communications. With the key word being *personal*, bank marketers began to humanize all their customer interactions. The bank had never before highlighted the people who worked at the bank. It hadn't done much in the way of showing customers in their messages. Because of the positioning, bank leaders determined to integrate real people into communications whenever possible. They decided to provide the emails and direct line phone numbers of the bank staff and team. The result was a human quality to their marketing that, although at the heart of the way the bank operates, had been missing from their messaging.

We helped the bank with an intensive photography project that captured each and every bank team member so they could be integrated into everything from print ads to a website directory. Knowing full well that the banking market is extremely competitive, the leaders knew that to succeed they had to present their people but also their competitive rates and product offerings. And the bank's rates and products were extremely competitive, often the best in the market. With this doubly strong proposition of people and product, we helped the bank develop the tagline, "Numbers. People." This line allowed the bank to simultaneously advertise everything from rates and lender phone numbers to photos of the lenders themselves and the people benefiting from their loans and products.

This combination placed the bank in a very strong position, but the icing on the cake was the fact that the bank was the only independent, member-owned bank in the community. So not only could customers count on a banking relationship with professionals they knew on a first name basis and a portfolio of products and rates that improved their financial health and well-being, they could do it with a financial institution totally invested in the community. This bank isn't a branch; it is the tree.

The Tools

The name, Home Savings Bank, is perfect because they do in fact call their community "home." The key tools created for the bank based on its cause and positioning included a totally new look for its print and magazine ads, brochures, business cards, newspaper wraps, website, product naming and icons, lobby materials and signage, event graphics and all other appropriate media, from outdoor to radio.

Internally, the bank truly embraced the cause of *personally helping*. Leaders made sure when a customer called the bank she spoke to a person, not a computer. They made sure when customers entered the bank, everyone was personally helped, regardless of whether they had giant deposits or just happened to wander into the lobby. They created access points for customers to reach a real person. They made sure that they continually bolstered the "personally help" cause of the bank by giving the bank staff and team the tools and cultural atmosphere necessary to really help the customers, the community, and their associates in a personal way.

To help make the community a better place, the bank introduced a green checking product and is also constructing a bank office that is environmentally friendly. This facility is the only certified green bank in the region. The construction of the building recycled virtually all the materials from the area in which it was erected. The building will feature alternative energy sources (as does another of their facilities) and will also include rain gardens as part of the building landscaping. The bank will showcase the building as a model for other businesses to follow as well as a springboard for educating customers on sustainability. This project is consistent with the bank's 100-plus years of investing in the community. And in every instance, you get the genuine feeling that the bank's leaders and employees take it all personally.

Three high concept campaigns designed to capture the "personally help" cause and positioning. Layouts are all conceptual and images are used for layout purposes only.

First Name Basis Concept

Messages begin with first names of bank associates ("Susan") and are punctuated with the tagline: "Financial freedom on a first name basis."

John saves more than money banking here. Because our new East Side location was built with sustainable materials and total energy efficiency in mind, he saves the environment with every visit. And—because the indoor air quality and abundance of natural light has increased productivity—John saves time, too. Stop by for a visit. 4820 East Washington Avenue.

Financial **freedom** on a **first-name** basis.

HOME
SavingsBank

Once messaging seeds the first-name-basis concept by introducing bank associates and customers ("John"), the campaign can begin to introduce products and benefits on a first name basis ("Home"—*commitment to the community*) and ("5.23%"—*home mortgage rates*).

Home is where the heart of independent banking is. In the Madison area since 1895, we've personally helped generations of customers (neighbors, friends, family) build a better life here. And we're all the better for it. Stop by. Say hi. We're Home.

Financial **freedom** on a **first-name** basis.

HOME
SavingsBank

5.23% can speak for itself as a 15-year fixed loan rate. But it can never listen. That's why, as proud as we are to offer competitive rates, our truest pride comes from the personal service that only we can deliver. We're Dane County's only depositor-owned full service bank. You can count on us in more ways than one.

Financial **freedom** on a **first-name** basis.

HOME
SavingsBank

Visit **www.goodforbusiness.com/book** for additional examples of this and other campaigns.

It's Personal Here Concept

Concept presents actual community landmarks as visual confirmers that this bank is in fact a local bank. Headlines and copy support the personal knowledge and relationship the bank has with the community. This particular message shows the bank's downtown headquarters with the headline: "We're the tree. Not the branch." Messages are punctuated with the tagline: "It's personal here."

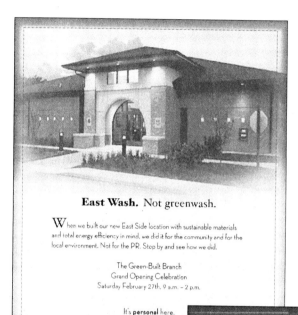

The concept tells the story of how the bank is investing in the community by building the only "green" banking facility in the state. Located on East Washington Avenue, the headline reads: "East Wash. Not Greenwash."

East Wash. Not greenwash.

When we built our new East Side location with sustainable materials and total energy efficiency in mind, we did it for the community and for the local environment. Not for the PR. Stop by and see how we did.

The Green-Built Branch
Grand Opening Celebration
Saturday February 27th, 9 a.m. – 2 p.m.

It's **personal** here.

HOME
SavingsBank

Messages present the bank's personal relationship with local businesses. This concept shows a community business called "Miles Away" and talks about how Home Savings Bank serves their needs.

Miles Away. Not miles away.

To us, Stoughton is a community, not a business opportunity. That's why when you step into our office—just 3 short blocks from the only singing waitstaff in town—you'll feel right at home.

It's **personal** here.

HOME
SavingsBank

Numbers. People. Selected Campaign Concept

You can always count on us for the most competitive rates. (Currently, we're offering a 15-year fixed mortgage rate of **5.23%** with a **5.284%** APR.)

But you can depend on all of us for more.

We are independent, customer-owned, and committed—since 1895—to keeping our community a great place to be.

Together, we are Home.

5.23%

Numbers. **People.**

HOME
SavingsBank

Numbers. **People.**

Numbers. **People.**

HOME
SavingsBank

Concept captures the two strengths of the bank—its people and its strong rates. This first conceptual message presents an image of a bank associate and a competitive rate with the headline: "Numbers. People." This headline serves as the tagline for the campaign as well.

The concept translates well to all kinds of tools from brochures (shown here) to website and electronic marketing.

Visit **www.goodforbusiness.com/book** for additional examples of this and other campaigns.

Sustainable. Investment.

Our brand-new East Side building was built sustainably from the ground up. (What else would you expect from an independent local bank that's been around for as long as we have?)

Green-Built Branch Open House and Info Session
Saturday, February 27th – 9am – 2pm.
Featuring our local partners—Madison Environmental Group and Linville Architects—and our brand-new "Dream in Green" 5% home improvement loan rate!

HOME SavingsBank

Numbers. People. campaign concept can expand to all types of connections. The message "Sustainable. Investment." talks about the bank's personal commitment to sustainability and the fact that its new "green" branch is 100 percent sustainable.

Lower than prime, our **5.75% APR FlexLine** home equity loan rate makes now the time to do what you want to do.

So, let's do it.

Call 282-6000 today.

HOME SavingsBank
Numbers. People.

Prime. Time.

Prime.Time. champions the bank's support of personal relationships (parent and child playing) and a very attractive prime rate (5.75%).

Family. History.

It makes perfect sense that a great place to raise children would be an ideal place to grow an independent bank like ours.

We've personally helped generations of customer-owners build financial health and freedom here for 110 years. And we've only just begun.

Together, we are Home.

HOME SavingsBank
Numbers. People.

The bank's commitment to the "family" customer base also presents the bank's commitment to family since its founding in 1895. This message also captures the "Numbers. People." concept, but with a broader appeal of "people" and a mission-based connection to "numbers."

FOUR

A Developer Who Doesn't Build Buildings

THIS MISSION-IN-A-MESSAGE encounter was unlike any other in the sense that rather than gathering around a table or in a setting conducive to conversation about cause and purpose, we made ourselves comfortable in the CEO's car and took off for a tour of the company's properties.

It was here that the president of the development company, T. Wall Properties, revealed his real passion and joy. As we went from one property to the next, I could see and hear the core vision driving the business. It was a vision that was already within the company, but just needed an experience like this to unearth and validate the *why* of the business. I tapped into the absolute pride and passion of the CEO as we walked through the company's new urbanism developments. From the kind of high quality stone and concrete materials to the artwork on the walls and design treatments, I felt his visionary entrepreneurship coming to terms with a heartfelt concern about the legacy of the business.

This development company likes creating something tangible. They like to bring it all together much like the producer of a show. There is a strong drive to connect things. Most of the competition's office buildings were just that, buildings that you go to work in and only work in. The buildings could be very cold. They could be aloof. There wasn't a vision to make the buildings in office parks truly relate to one another. Instead, they seemed to be just plopped down amidst the most sterile of landscaping. There wasn't much respect for walking or the natural setting. This sense of architectural detachment in most business parks is in contrast to this company's leadership's desire to create environments that are integrated, livable, human, people-oriented and holistic. They want to create environments, not just buildings, that bring people together. They want to have people be happy in their environment, to be satisfied, and comfortable, yet inspired. They believe buildings should not be commodities, but they should actually enhance the flow of life. They want to set new standards that completely transcend the attitude of just building buildings. There exists in this business a strong commitment that if they can't do it this way, they just won't do it. People and buildings should be married in harmony.

Along with this drive to create environments where people connect, what else makes up the DNA of the company? I found the leaders to be very intelligent, but in a down-to-earth way. They are refreshingly honest, creative, spirited, passionate, fearless, instinctive, and use common sense. This business loves the saying "The difference between a stumbling block and a steppingstone is a matter of character; some people see risk, others see opportunity. Guess what we see?" They offer tremendous opportunity and responsibility to their employees. They want their people to grow. They want them to derive a satisfaction from doing a great job.

They believe this kind of work environment helps them create tangible experiences and *integrated environments*. They aim to build human, people-oriented places that enhance the quality and flow of life, environments that are satisfying, comfortable, and create no points of negative friction. This is why they exist. They want to create places where people are actually happy to be. They referred to the idea of creating places that give back something that has been lost. From all this, their cause revealed itself to be:

We create places for human interaction to occur

They see this to be their cause both internally and externally. This kind of interaction should occur within the walls of the business itself, in the properties they create, in the relationships they have with customers, contractors, and community. Their business actually becomes a force for creating positive interactions at all levels, inside and out. This cause catalyzes innovation, creativity, and meaning. The interaction they are defining reflects the key values of the company's properties: Intelligence, Creativity, Honesty, and Passion.

The company's executives realized that their customers, shareholders, vendors, and associates all have to buy into the cause and that communicating their cause is an act that directly reflects their goal of creating interaction. Telling this story transcends commodity thinking. Their story has an educational aspect to it. It needs to be told as a means of inspiring and providing a role model to others. They had been a quiet company, but being quiet about this cause would do everyone a disservice. Their communications should actually create places for human interaction to occur.

Their communications need to address several key audiences: their employees, vendors, contractors, customers (CEOs, CFOs and people making office decisions), brokers, investors, strategic partners, and government officials. With all these audiences they want to create value-based, win-win relationships. But at the core of their message is the need to speak to that core customer who makes the final decision on a deal. This customer could be a CEO, broker, or plumber. This customer is typically male, but the female segment of this audience is growing. Many are national and regional, so the messages can't assume they are familiar with the company or the community. Many are actual managers of businesses. They typically think visually rather than verbally. They could be in wingtips or blue jeans. Many of the brokers are young and male, often times entry-level and they need to understand the value and flexibility of the development company.

The Barriers

What's standing in the way of communicating their cause? Well, let's start with bureaucracies, including the government. They are in a business where a lot of selling is only based on price and selling that is only based on price neglects and avoids the value of their proposition. There are Neanderthal attitudes about development and conventional thinking and mindsets that say it's "just a building." There is the attitude that developers are big and bad. This industry has a resistance to breaking the mold. Economic issues such as changing interest rates and demands for space can stand in the way. More specifically, the perception of this developer is one that is aggressive, young, won't accept no, and it is not part of establishment.

What does this company have, besides a vision and belief that will allow them to truly fulfill its cause and promise of creating places where people interact? It does have a proven track record and can demonstrate business environments it has developed where human interaction is the driving force behind the blueprints and backhoe. The company doesn't build sterile buildings. Its environments are home to all kinds of businesses. From concerts performed at lunch on the plaza to state-of-the-art conference rooms, dynamic lobbies and natural landscaping to coffee shops, libraries, bike paths, fitness centers, retail, hotels, restaurants, skywalks, artwork and warm colors, its properties embrace the vision of a village. This developer makes the term *new urbanism* very real. Not only is it pioneering, but also it is setting a new standard for development in the region. From a practical point of view, it accommodates its customers' growth and expansion. It offers creative financing and flexible leasing opportunities. Just as its environments create interaction, the company's employees continually interact with their customers to make sure they are delighted. By owning and maintaining their own buildings, they have an inherent sense of pride in their work and think of people first, then profit. The environments they create actually contribute to employee retention. They improve productivity. They spark innovation. It's not about the building; it's about the people. They work from a human blueprint from which everyone can benefit.

The Cause and Its Effect

T. Wall Properties engaged us at a critical juncture in the company's life. It was growing significantly and with the growth came the typical tension between staying the course and entrepreneurial opportunities, between growing a culture of an ever-expanding workforce and the entrepreneurial leanings of the leader and founder of the company. The leader of the company was at a point in his career where he realized he was definitely creating something bigger than himself. He acknowledged that there was a sense of legacy in what the company was doing. After all, developers build things, and those things are usually seen by the community and become monuments and testaments to the values and dreams of the community. This developer was at the point where he not only wanted to crystallize and clarify the purpose and proposition of his business, but to do so in way that would leave a positive and inspiring legacy. The key outcome of our Mission in a Message process was the realization that the company wasn't just about building buildings. It was about creating places where people interact. Up until this point, the messages of the company were traditional. The ads and brochures showed pretty pictures of buildings, but often absent of humanity. Or their ads showed images of the founder of the company, perhaps with him shaking the hand of a customer/client. The Message-in-a-Mission process completely transformed this approach.

The key word of T. Wall Properties' communications strategy is *people*. With that, people are the centerpiece of its new communications, and not just static images of people, but people interacting. Instead of showing beautiful buildings, the messages show people doing what they do inside and outside those beautiful buildings. The communications capture the way the buildings celebrate humanity and encourage interaction at every turn. And nowhere in the core communication materials will the founder be seen front and center. The heroes of this campaign are the people who are spending their waking and working moments in the buildings this company creates. The communications show how its developments embrace new urbanism by having the buildings relate in a positive way with the landscape and environment. The need to drive a car is minimized. The brochures and ads show landscapes with bike and walking paths and creeks and a respect for the natural surroundings. There are plazas and gathering places. There are shops and restaurants that make the work experience more of a balanced life experience and put much of what workers want right at their office doorsteps.

The company's approach to this kind of interactive development was acknowledged with the region's top architecture and design award. Messages shared this news. The company culture took the mantra of interaction seriously, too. Management practices have been adopted that enhance worker interaction and communication. Physical space has been designed and accented to facilitate employee interaction. The company executives realize that this process is a journey and getting to where they want to be won't happen overnight. The key is the fact that they are committed to this journey. Communication tools created to begin to tell this story include the development of a new logo and tagline; a corporate capability brochure; individual property brochures; presentation materials; a new business-to-business advertising campaign; new signage; annual report; newsletter; video and interactive website, and more. Like many who invest in cause-based communications, pillars support the proposition. The pillars of T. Wall Properties are community, confidence, creativity, convenience, comfort, and flexibility. Naturally, I couldn't resist capturing the company's proposition and pillars accordingly:

Wall to wall confidence

Wall to wall community

Wall to wall creativity

Wall to wall convenience

Wall to wall flexibility

Wall to wall comfort

The testament to how the communications brief we developed refocused not just the messaging but the company occurred when the founder gave the acceptance speech upon receiving the top design/development award. His opening remark was, "It's not about the building; it's about the people." This represented an authentic shift of communications strategy, on paper and in person.

Conceptual campaigns designed to capture the "creating places where people interact" cause and positioning. Layouts are conceptual only and images are for layout purposes only. Visit **www.goodforbusiness.com/book** for additional examples of this and other campaigns.

Interactions, If I, and *Wall to Wall One* **Concepts**

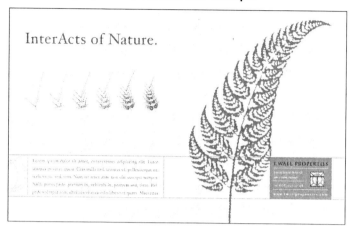

This concept captures the interaction theme via bold images that symbolize interaction and connection and ties those images into the key attributes and strengths of the client's value proposition.

This campaign concept approach visually juxtaposes customers, property and specific benefits. Customers, captured as "people close-ups," express their "If I were a developer" dreams and desires.

This concept integrates the client name into the actual messaging. This "Wall to Wall" option employs single bold images that express the company's complete and comprehensive commitment to values such as community.

Wall to Wall Selected Campaign

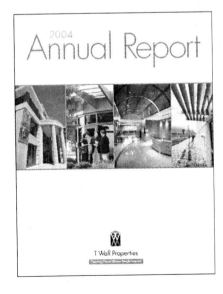

Concept also integrates client name into the actual messaging and visually displays a "wall-to-wall" effect. Rather than a single bold image, a series of supporting images are aligned between two inviting walls. The supporting images reinforce values and features such as creativity, community, comfort and flexibility. This theme is applied to everything from the annual report to the website.

A new logo was created for the client based on the new positioning and cause: *creating places where people interact.*

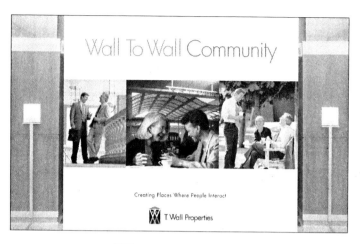

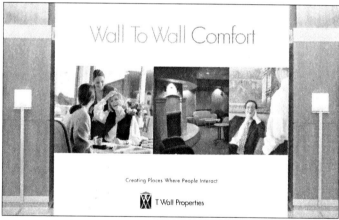

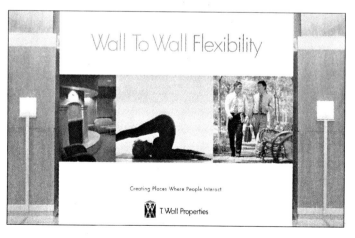

FIVE

Drawing Out the Cause of a Non-profit

WHEN I ASKED the board, executive director, representative members and staff, why their statewide assembly of local artists existed, the unabashed response was "Change the world!" Upon hearing that, I knew I was working with a dynamic, passionate group and this was going to be fun (yes, we said the "f-word"—another old-school business no-no!)

I then asked what would happen if this organization didn't exist. They said it would be disastrous for the artists and their local arts groups. A fragmentation would occur that isolates communities. A powerful connection to the legislature would disappear. There would most likely be a shift to individual need rather than the common good. Rather than this organization's rising tide lifting all boats, local organizations would sink. The clout and muscle resulting from this group's collective would vanish. Networking opportunities would decrease as would access to key resources, education and technology.

From metropolitan symphonies to the rural sculptor, this organization helps all artists understand they are connected and that every community benefits from incorporating arts and culture. If this organization is truly for social change, it needs to figure out how to impact the communities in which it operates. To do this, it needs not only the artists and the arts community, but the door should be open to allow all people who care about their communities to be involved.

This is not just about getting the Wisconsin state funds necessary for the arts; this organization has got to be about raising the bar for public and private support for the arts. The members care about the community. They care about creativity. They believe it is what makes us human. This is the emotional connect; this is the power of art.

So, is their true mission to raise money for arts purposes—public dollars, lobbying arts foundations, advocating for arts purposes, and matching resources to the arts or artist? Is their purpose to become a political organization with muscle? Do they want to put more emphasis on education?

I asked them again *why* they exist? Why do they want to change the world? What I heard was that these organizational members believe with all their heart in the power of the arts to transform the human condition. They believe that creating and experiencing art is essential to being human and that this experience can change people for the better, which, in turn, makes communities better. They believe their region will thrive and flourish through the arts. They believe every child and every adult deserves the arts and needs an outlet to be creative. In other words, they believe everyone in their state should have access to the arts. No, I take that back. They believe everyone in their state *will* have access to the arts. And their cause is:

"To make sure everyone here experiences the arts."

This organization operates at the intersection of community and economic development. It combines grassroots and political muscle to be effective. It is the connector of arts, politics, and business. It advocates and educates for increasing resources for arts purposes. It is an agent of change. It gives power to the arts by getting power from the arts.

Part of its educational mission is to make sure that everyone understands all the diverse, creative things available in the state, that no matter where you live or what you do, you can always have an "art experience." The arts make us human and it's this group's responsibility to be the action organization, or advocates for this humanizing experience. The group realizes that its mission is to advocate for the arts so that everyone can experience the arts.

What's standing in their way? These are the negative forces currently facing the arts. State arts organizations are more artistically creative and more organizationally mature and fiscally responsible than ever, but are becoming victims of their own success. The number of applications for arts board funding continues to increase in Wisconsin's thriving arts environment. However, as the funding available remains stagnant, the amount of money awarded and the number of community-based programs and projects funded are decreasing. This leads to organizations cutting back on the number and scope of their programming. The result is fewer cultural opportunities for residents. When it comes to per-capita funding for the arts, Wisconsin ranks 44th out of 50 states, according to a survey by the National Assembly of State Arts Agencies. State arts agencies are an excellent investment for state government, providing services to a broad constituent base while accounting for an average of only .087 percent of states' general funds nationwide.

Wisconsin's funding of the arts has declined significantly in the past ten years. Over the past decade, the State Arts Board's GPR (General Purpose Revenue, or tax dollars) funding has declined by more than 23 percent while the budgets of statewide projects recommended for funding by qualified review panels have tripled. The gap between the amounts requested by applicants deemed eligible by peer panels and the amount of money available was $4 million. This number will get progressively worse, because of the success of state arts organizations, the arts facilities building and remodeling boom, and inflation. In addition, a state budget crisis (a $1.17 billion deficit) will surely further diminish an already-inadequate state arts budget. State arts organizations pay 5 percent sales tax on tickets sold for live performances. Wisconsin is the only state in the region requiring its arts organizations to pay sales tax. This tax burden has a ceiling effect on the amount that can be charged for a ticket and the dollars available for reinvestment in the organization's charitable mission. Tracking and reporting this information is also a burden.

While a new or renovated facility development is extremely exciting, it highlights an urgent challenge to our communities in the 21st century: how to sustain the facilities once they are built, and how to fund and grow the cultural programming that serves the community. The private sector tends to enthusiastically fund bricks and mortar projects, and government plays a critical role by providing support for the artistic activities that will fill the buildings when open. The arts are facing a double punch in funding cuts. In addition to possible cuts in funding from the State Arts Board, local arts organizations and cultural centers are facing possible cuts in funding from their towns, cities, and counties, meaning a reduction in services to their constituents.

Not a pretty picture. But, despite the obstacles, especially financial ones, this arts advocacy organization has a lot of strengths and power in its story. It is the only organization serving the entire arts and cultural community through advocacy, education, information, research, and technical assistance. It is politically active and astute and provides the necessary "art muscle" to make good things happen. It supports and promotes legislative programs and policy initiatives that benefit the arts in Wisconsin. It provides advocacy, technical assistance, training, and convenes the arts industry for all kinds of strategic initiatives, from decreasing brain drain, expanding on the 8,000 businesses and 43,000 jobs generated by the arts to leveraging over $500 million in private investment and $290 million in economic activity to building a "creative economy." It empowers artists and arts organizations to be community leaders and gives them tools to be advocates. It's a long-term organization, helping the arts find sustainable funding and making sure they have the tools to keep going instead of reacting to one financial crisis after another. The

Wisconsin Assembly for Local Arts holds forums and workshops to bring together arts, business, education, government and civic leaders to envision and act on Wisconsin's economic, educational and civic future.

The Cause and Its Effect

This is a membership organization led by an enthusiastic, passionate, positively contagious executive director. The organization was in the midst of doing classic business and organizational strategic planning when they brought us into the picture. The timing couldn't have been better. The organization was at a crossroads in terms of defining itself, building on the strengths of its leadership, and tapping into the muscle and power of its members. The Mission-in-a-Message experience revealed that the organization's message had been a bit fractured and pulled in different directions in order to capitalize on all kinds of opportunities. There also was confusion between this organization and another statewide arts organization, so some clarity needed to be established there as well.

I found out what made this organization different from the one they were confused with and that discovery set the stage for the new positioning. They realized that they were the only organization in the state committed to the well-being of all artists as well as all citizens throughout the state through their experience of the arts. They were the advocate for the arts and the artist and were known for their "Arts Day" where artists and patrons converged on the capitol to lobby for the arts. They were activists. They were creative. They were smart.

The cause they embraced "to ensure everyone in Wisconsin will experience the arts" was right on. This cause prompted the organization to change its name from the often-misquoted "Wisconsin Assembly for Local Arts" to simply "Arts Wisconsin." To substantiate the drive to clarity, the name was punctuated with a simple tagline: "Everyone. Everywhere."

Instead of taking three or four paragraphs to explain who it is, what it does and why it does it, Arts Wisconsin had it all in four words. We created a new logo, new brochure, new website, new e-letters, and other materials that suddenly put it on the map as a force to be respected and reckoned with (not that it wasn't before, it's just that its communications got in the way of the force). This new positioning made so much of an impact that the state's leading business publication stepped forward as Arts Wisconsin's partner in championing the arts and creative economy. The publication offered a full year campaign of free ad space and supporting editorial. It also hosted a creative economy roundtable where participants included the executive director of Arts Wisconsin, the Lieutenant Governor and economists and business leaders from around the state. The roundtable discussion was inserted into the publication and distributed statewide. Because of this partnership, we helped Arts Wisconsin create a supporting campaign that told the story about the economic impact of the arts. The campaign was based on the premise that you don't know what you have until it's gone. Based on this premise, we took classic business phrases and terms and removed three key letters—A, R, and T—from them to create headlines that read:

QU   ERLY PROFITS

BUSINESS P   NER

SM   T WORKFORCE

ICLES OF INCORPORATION

With this concept, we developed business-to-business ads, web banner ads, TV spots, postcards, and posters, then made the materials available to member organizations throughout the state. The campaign caught the eye of the national organization "Americans for the Arts" which had just brought "Business in the Arts" under its wing. The campaign is being considered now as the national message for the economic impact of the arts. And, Wisconsin is scheduled to host the 2006 national conference of state arts organizations.

Approach each new problem not with a view of finding what you hope will be there, but to get to the truth, the realities that must be grappled with. You may not like what you find. In that case you are entitled to try to change it. But do not deceive yourself as to what you do find to be the facts of the situation.

Bernard Baruch

Arts Wisconsin

SM   WORKFORCE

ARTS WISCONSIN

everyone everywhere

You don't know what you have 'til it's gone.

Without the A R T s, Wisconsin would lose a lot of brains and brawn. Our knowledge workers would wander off to labor with love in more inspiring and $290 million of annual economic muscle would simply shrink away.

Join us in keeping the arts with us always. Things work a lot better with them. Visit **artswisconsin.org** today for your free *Business & Arts Handbook*.

ARTS WISCON

everyone everywhere

QU   ERLY PROFITS

You don't know what you have 'til it's gone.

Without the A R T s, Wisconsin would lose 8,050 related businesses and 43,568 jobs. We'd be down $290 million in economic activity annually. And your ability to attract talent to your company and your community would suffer significantly.

Join us in committing to keep the arts throughout Wisconsin. Because without it, nothing makes much sense.

Visit **artswisconsin.org** today for your free *Business & Arts Handbook*.

ARTS WISCONSIN

everyone everywhere

BUSINESS P   NERS

You don't know what you have 'til it's gone.

Without the A R T s, forward-thinking corporations would overlook Wisconsin when deciding where to go and grow. (And who can blame them?) And we can't leave out the fact $290 million in economic activity is generated annually by our arts and cultural organizations.

Join us in keeping the arts with us always. Because without them, what do we really have to offer? Visit **artswisconsin.org** today for your free *Business & Arts Handbook*.

ARTS WISCONSIN

everyone everywhere

New name, identity, tagline and business awareness campaign created based on the cause: "to make sure everyone here experiences the arts."

Business awareness campaign includes print/trade ads, web banner ads, TV, billboards, and cause-marketing opportunities.

Arts Wisconsin

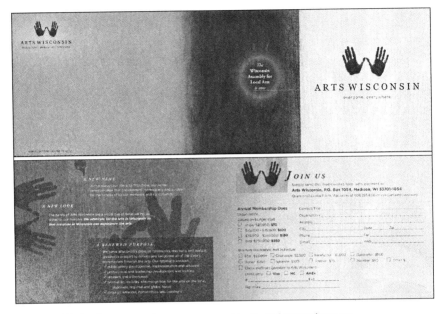

Membership brochure announcing new name, new identity and renewed purpose.

A website based on the new positioning and cause was created as well as other tools ranging from a "Business Handbook" to buttons and clocks.

SIX

Community Is the Fuel of this Utility

FOR OVER 100 YEARS, MGE (Madison Gas & Electric) has been serving its community by providing electricity and natural gas. Unlike other energy companies that have an unusual compulsion to diversify into areas remotely related to energy, this utility has stayed true to its knitting in terms of providing reliable, affordable energy. The lights go on. The houses are heated. The businesses produce. But this energy company has made a point to plug itself in all kinds of programs and initiatives designed to make the community a better place. And they haven't done this in an Enron way—a way that is all window-dressing or detached from an unhealthy leadership core. This company's community commitment comes from a leadership core that is healthy and enlightened. For over a century, this company has involved itself in improving everything from the public education program and planting trees to championing business incubators and developing alternative, renewable energy. It is a good business doing good things. *Business Ethics* consistently ranks it as one of the country's top 100 corporate citizens. But its managers found that they were having difficulty framing all their good work within the context of their core value proposition of affordable, reliable energy. Part of it was due to the Midwestern roots of the company and the uncomfortable feeling Midwesterners have in letting the world know about their positive contributions. Part of it was due to the realization that if they were going to let the world know about their positive contributions, that message must be completely true and unquestionable. This combination was ideal for a cause-based communications program. And so our relationship began.

MGE wanted to tell all its stakeholders that it was the community's energy company. But it wanted to be sure what this promise actually meant. Together, we began to look at all the things MGE did for the community. We found activities and initiatives that were seemingly endless and began to construct working lists of community programs. It became evident that MGE could authentically make this claim, but the claim needed to be grounded and focused. The Mission-in-a-Message process provided such focus. In fact, the Mission-in-a-Message process provided six points of focus and clarity.

We created an umbrella core strategy as well as five supporting strategies that built the core. Each one of these supporting strategies is called a pillar. The five pillars constructed the core strategy. The core strategy was based on the company cause:

"To be held responsible for the community and its energy."

Because the cause is to be held responsible for the community and its energy, inherently, it would be irresponsible for the **energy company** to not tell its story. Without communicating, it can't be credible or accountable. The community looks to it for explanations. The managers realize that telling their story carries with it a component of listening as well.

They also realize they have obstacles, everything from their size (as a company they are small) and rates perceptions to customer desires for renewable energy, transmission restraints, the complicated nature of their product, deregulation, and their visibility in the community. In spite of all that stands in their way, they have a great, true story to tell.

The executives are serious about their responsibility to provide energy for this community. They are more than pipes and wires. As the community energy company, they are committed to improving the quality of life for all of who live and work here—to make the lights shine, warm homes, and help businesses run reliably. They take responsibility to plan and provide a reliable energy supply that balances the needs and values of those they serve. They provide information and education to serve customers and stakeholders and help inform their energy decisions. They preserve and protect the environment while providing affordable, reliable energy. They encourage and support business and community development to keep the economy strong and vibrant. They engage in open, honest dialogue, in partnership and collaboration to best serve customers and the broader community. They listen. From workshops, seminars and exhibits to open houses, neighborhood eco-teams, brochures, and up-to-the-minute online information and knowledge, they continually connect, inform and learn. It's been their privilege to serve the community for more than 100 years. They hope that citizens believe this community is a better place because they are here.

The leaders profiled their voice as unadorned and straightforward. It's transparent, not hidden. It's bold, clean and colorful. They are real—real places, people, and programs. Their voice is colorful rather than black and white. They're green. They are authentic and unpretentious, truthful and sincere, pleasant and caring. They're regular, familiar. And "take your shoes off" comfortable. They are more visual than verbal.

MGE's Cause and Its Effect

For years, leaders at the energy company had wondered how to tell their story in a consistent and compelling way. They had a rich and reputable history of taking responsibility for their community and its energy. But how to tell that story needed to be addressed. The Mission-in-a-Message process helped them focus, clarify and create a roadmap for communicating their complex message. The company's tagline, "Your community energy company," definitely captured who it was and what it wanted to be. The executives wanted to be sure the message was truly authentic and they wanted to see if it could be their core proposition for years to come. I found out that it indeed was authentic and that they could own this promise in perpetuity, as long as they continued to be committed to their century-long values. Together we created an umbrella Mission in a Message that served as the foundation for all marketing communications. We then explored the pillars of the company that made their core proposition true. We found five powerful pillars they could build on and constructed sub-Mission-in-a-Message strategies for each pillar. You can see in the communication samples provided here that their key word is *responsible*. In their case, the key word is literally embedded in their communications and punctuates the five pillars. The 'e' in the MGE logo is linked with the 'e' at the end of the word *responsible*. In fact, an entire, unique MGE typeface based on the 'e' was created for MGE to tell its story.

The linked pillars look like this:

responsibl**e**nergy

responsibl**e**nvironment

responsibl**e**ducation

responsibl**e**ngagement

responsibl**e**conomy

The pillars serve as the pockets for communications. They are all built according to tight corporate standards and guidelines so there is absolute consistency in message and the opportunity to build message equity is always present. Yet, each of these pillars stands on its own as it addresses distinct initiatives and programs undertaken by MGE. The umbrella brochure communicates the fact that it is the community's energy company and then shows how each pillar supports that fact. Sub-brochures are created for each pillar and sub-sub-brochures for initiatives within each pillar. In all cases the look, voice, and feel of the materials is totally consistent. Whether we are talking about how MGE invests in the economy or how it helps sustain the environment, the messaging stays true to the core voice and personality we helped capture for the company.

The tools created to date that embrace this plan include its core brochures; supporting brochures; rack brochures on over 50 subjects from winter heating to energy efficient appliances; exhibits and displays for the core positioning as well as displays for each of the five pillars; new photography that helps capture the idea of *responsible*; community workshops and conversations; a new website; bill stuffers; print ads; bus signs; billboards, radio and television ads; web banner ads; program sponsorships; and funding of aligned community projects, such as the Aldo Leopold conservation program and awards to start-up business incubators. Also included are speaker's kits, community outreach tools, and more. We also embraced the green the company has been known for and has integrated into all its messaging, again, to provide it with ownership of its authentic promise and also to control the consistency and continuity of communications. Internally there wasn't a need for the culture to go through responsible training. The culture and workforce had already been living this promise.

There was the need, though, for the culture to see and realize the importance of telling its story with clarity and consistency. Whether it is at a neighborhood eco-team meeting or a shareholders' meeting, MGE has truly woven its responsible message into the fabric of the community. It has also refocused its communications in a way that is completely information-based. Its advertising provides customers with tips and ways of saving energy. It develops campaigns that talk about the financial and environmental benefits of energy conservation and devotes 95 percent of the ad space to this information. The messages are virtually egoless and void of self-congratulation and serve as a premier example of socially responsible communications. Imagine, an energy company actually encouraging people to use less of its product.

Outdoor billboard and transit bus sign from multi-media energy conservation campaign.

The "community energy company" campaign has been integrated in all communication tools—from conservation television, radio, print and web messaging to exhibits, bill stuffers, rack brochures and community energy workshops. Here is an example of an outdoor billboard and transit bus sign from the multi-media "turn back thermostat" energy conservation campaign.

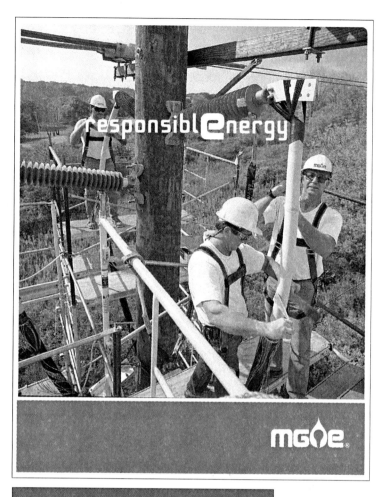

Cover of MGE Responsible Energy brochure.

Banner/ transit/poster concepts for energy efficiency and safety initiatives.

Covers of new home planning energy efficiency guide and of comprehensive brochure explaining MGE's commitment to being the community's energy company.

Core images for three of MGE's "*esponsible*" pillars: *environment, economy* and *education*. The two other responsible pillars, *energy* and *engagement* are also supported by a full array of communication tools.

Visit **www.goodforbusiness.com/book** for additional examples of this and other campaigns.

SEVEN
How to Why

THE MISSION-IN-A-MESSAGE process consists of ten questions, shown on the next page. Chapter Two went into detail about Question One and why it is the most significant question. Here are some thoughts on the other nine questions that you will find helpful in creating your own Mission in a Message.

Why Tell Your Truth?

Answering this question will accomplish a number of things for your organization. First, it will give more concrete form to the passion of your cause. It would be tragic to unearth and validate the purpose of your organization and then let all the power that lives in your cause go into hibernation.

Some businesses and organizations call themselves quiet. That's just fine. But just because you are the quiet type doesn't mean you never express yourself. You express yourself in a quiet way, but you don't become a marketing wallflower and disappear into the wood-work. Being totally silent won't do you much good in the long run. Eventually the fear that pushes you to censor your story will silence your business. If you accept the proposition that you are a cause to be believed in, there is no room for fear. Doing business as a cause requires courage.

Telling your story isn't about bragging or being a self-absorbed bore. It's a matter of letting the world know who you are, what you do, and why you do it. Without this information, the world will have a difficult time noticing you and trusting you. Telling your story from a place of cause is telling the truth. Telling the truth is not tooting your horn. If you don't tell your story, who will? Being listed in the phone book isn't going to cut it, especially when you realize your business is a cause for good. You will be amazed at how hungry your customers, employees, and community are for businesses to honestly connect with them. Such honesty inspires and creates a kinship that will stand all kinds of tests. It's an amazement that leads to rewards.

Answering this question brings to the surface all the hesitations and resentment an organization may have toward marketing and communications. This part of the conversation can get heated and testy. That's okay. What you are doing is redefining communications. It's no longer just making ads and selling something. You now realize communication is the primary tool for building trust both inside and outside your business. You realize communication is the most powerful force in the world today and it's part of your role in both society and business to make sure you make it a force for good. That good can be educating and enlightening your markets, improving the station in life of your customers, or making the communities you have contact with better places to live, work, and play. So be bold. Leave no stone unturned. Talk about what hasn't been talked about before. Challenge all the resistance to telling your story. Reflect on that resistance and turn it into strength.

Answering the Question

The most fascinating part of this question is the process of answering it. The process itself is the act of communicating. How it's acted upon will speak volumes about your organization. It's this question and how you answer it that will be the lubricant for your "cause engine." If the communications revolving around this question are forthright, challenging, bold, and transparent, your communications should sing, or at least, hum.

Mission in a Message: Communicating Cause

1 Your True Cause

"Why" does your business or organization do "what" it does? Why does it exist? What would the world and your community be like if it didn't exist or were to leave?

2 Why Tell Your Truth

What will communicating your cause accomplish for your business? This is not about blowing your horn, it's about telling your story.

3 Tell "Me" the Truth

Who are your audiences? Who is your primary audience? What do you know about them? What do they know about you?

4 What's Stopping You from Telling The Truth

What is the competitive climate? What is being said by others? What are the emotional, psychological, political and economic obstacles in your way?

5 What's Truly in It for Them

What is the key benefit you can provide to your key audience? Your value proposition? What is the principal idea that underlies all your communication?

6 True To One's Word

What single word captures your benefit and primary idea? Yes, one word! (This word needs to be present in your value proposition—Question 5.)

7 A Matter of Facts

Why should people believe you? What are the support points and facts that validate your proposition? Why should your primary benefit be trusted?

8 Cause for Action

What is the desired action? What do you want your audience to do? What are you trying to achieve when they hear your story?

9 Your True Voice

What is the character and personality of your cause? Your true colors? What does your cause look, taste, smell, feel and sound like? What's your style, your tone?

10 True to Form

What elements do you need to tell your story? Are you creating complete campaigns? Internal communications? Just a brochure?

Peter Drucker noted that business has only two functions, marketing and innovation. Answering this question will help your business fulfill its marketing function, and fulfill it in a way that transcends marketing as usual. If you agree with the definition of marketing as acquiring and keeping customers and that the acquisition requires strategies and tactics that will identify, manifest, and maintain healthy relationships that benefit and create value for you and your customers, then there is no option but to market yourself. What makes cause-based marketing so effective is that those relationships, whether they are internal with your team or external with your audiences, are born and reared with nothing but the truth. John D. Rockefeller ascribed to this principle: "Next to doing the right thing, the most important thing is to let people know you are doing the right thing." Well, your cause is your *right thing*. Now, it's a question of how you let your audiences know about it.

Answers to this question go from the blunt and direct to the more cerebral and philosophical. Have your leadership team talk about why they either jump at the chance to talk about the company to others, or why they crawl under a rock when the opportunity to speak about the business appears. Ask what would happen if there was no word of mouth around your business? What would happen if you didn't have a brochure or website or even a business card? What would happen if you didn't have a name for your business?

Whenever you bump into resistance to marketing or communications, try to find out where the resistance gets its energy. Listen to all the marketing war stories. Discuss crisis management related to marketing issues. Conduct an audit of all your communication efforts to see what worked, what didn't, and why. Talk about missed market opportunities because of the wallflower factor or mistrust of marketing. Get it all out. Then, begin to construct a working list of reasons why you need to tell your story.

You may not have to go into this kind of depth on this question if your organization is marketing friendly. If it is marketing friendly, make sure that friendliness comes from a place of truth and authenticity and not just golf trips to Maui as sales incentives, or an ad campaign that attacks competitors without saying a thing about your own company, or storytelling that smacks more of fiction than non-fiction. Once you have consensus on the cause and the reasons why communicating your cause is important to your success, move on to the next question.

> *Rather than love, than money, than fame, give me truth. I sat at a table where there were rich food and wine in abundance, and obsequious attendance, but sincerity and truth were not; and I went away hungry from the inhospitable board.*

Henry David Thoreau

Who Is Me? Why Tell Me The Truth?

When we ask, "Tell us who your audience is?" 99 percent of the time businesses claim they have many potential audiences. In fact, most of the time they have lists and categories of audiences. Certainly, from a marketing standpoint, it is important to be concerned about all the interests you have in telling your story, and there should be consistency when speaking to all those audiences. Yet, there are certain, primary audiences on which a business or organization needs to focus in order to achieve its cause and to be successful.

Not every business has either the financial or operational resources to create full-throttle, market-segmented messages. For practicality's sake and for the purpose of clarity, there is the need to identify a single key audience. This is the audience critical not only to maintaining your business position, but more importantly, for thriving into the future. I usually work with very realistic (i.e., tight) budgets and the need to be clear, efficient, and compelling with messages is paramount. So, I make the business or organization prioritize and commit. This is not to say we won't honor, respect, and try to reach all the other potential audiences. But it acknowledges, affirms, and acts upon knowing first and foremost with whom the cause-based business needs to connect for its cause to endure and advance.

Typically, businesses and organizations have done some research about audience and markets and I love looking into that data through the *cause* lens. This is where a kind of courage arises that isn't present in mainstream branding. Mainstream branding looks at external audiences and then shapes, manipulates, spins, and even contorts value propositions to fit what the external world wants and needs (or we should say what marketers think they need and want).

Cause communications respect the needs and wants of the external markets and customers, but that respect is always grounded by the internal and then externally championed cause. This approach to audience determination and customer engagement is based on the long view. It sits at the altar of authenticity and transparency and the fearless promise to the market. This promise is strong, confident and able to take on all kinds of whims, trends, and ups and downs. It's a promise that comes from both the heart and mind of a business and therefore speaks to the hearts and minds of its stakeholders in ways that transcend branding as usual.

Once you are grounded in your cause, it is crucial to understand your customers' needs and preferences. Your primary audience is a distinct group of customers (or stakeholders), and clearly defining this group will help you promote the story of your business that is most relevant to each group. But always remember, you aren't censoring or editing your story so it seems palatable to this group. You are championing your story with conviction and a confident, consistent voice. Strong marketing strategies will be pertinent and germane to all your customers, but understanding the primary audience well will help you deliver your messages in a way customers will respond to best.

Begin by breaking out and segmenting your existing customers and audiences. Who is your most profitable customer or audience? Who is the audience that composes the lion's share of your business? Is there a common thread among your audiences?

You can further analyze and divide your audiences according to demographics and psychographics. Demographics organize people according to things like age, location, occupation, sex and income. Psychographics profile audiences according to their interests and attitudes, like people who collect stamps or refinish furniture, or believe in supporting the arts. Now begin to ask questions about your customer such as their age range and median age? Are they male? Female? Do they live in the city or suburbs or rural area? What is their level of education? What are their hobbies? How much money do they make?

Understanding your audiences will assist you in combining key attributes and factors that end up defining your audiences with more specific profiles such as women, aged 25 to 34, one child, married, income of $35,000, lives in suburb, loves crafts and Italian food; or male, age 55 to 65, married, grandparent, income of $100,000, avid golfer and vacations in Arizona every year. Now, blend into these profiles beliefs, values, dreams, and principles. Once you define your audiences, you can begin to discover how your business or organization and its products relate to their values and beliefs. How can you get that intimate with them?

Talk with people who are actually in your primary audience. Speak with them about what they love and hate. Act like a researcher, or hire a researcher on this wavelength, and create an actual survey. Share the questions with your existing customers as well potential customers. Come up with an incentive for completing the questionnaire.

Ninety percent of our knowledge comes from listening, not talking. So imagine how much you can learn by tuning into the conversations and messages of your primary audience. Pay attention to what they say, and don't say, what they feel and repress, and you'll begin to paint a pretty accurate picture of what makes them tick. Hang out where your primary audience hangs out, from the grocery store to the neighborhood bar or soccer field. Where they spend their time will provide you with a snapshot of what's important to them and who is important in their lives.

As you unearth more about your primary audiences, make sure you document it and make the documentation as detailed and systematic as possible. This analysis will help you in all your communication efforts and planning. It can help you find ways to make your most profitable customers refer you to more customers, or increase the involvement and commitment of your primary audience with your product and service. See how this analysis not only reflects on your communication goals, but also your corporate objectives.

Using the information and understanding you've collected and analyzed about your primary audience, you can begin to determine how to best achieve your cause by creating one communications program to accommodate various audiences *even as you zero in* on the key single audience for your success.

The more thoroughly and distinctively you profile your primary audiences, the more effective you will be in connecting with them and having them tap into the passion and authenticity of your market proposition. As you track the effectiveness of your marketing efforts, set up a means to continually update, enhance, refresh, and direct your audience data. Preferences and business climates are constantly moving and shifting, and the most successful business leaders are those who adapt their businesses to those constant changes, yet always with clear focus on the cause.

Along with the classic audience analysis, the process of a business determining its primary audience requires doses of both courage and reality. It requires the business to be comfortable in its own skin and not controlled by the need to be all things to all people. It also demands that the business come to grips with the fact that there is a group out there that will profoundly influence the well-being of the business. This isn't a confirmation of the rule that "the customer is always right" or the "customer always comes first." The businesses I have the honor of working with realize the "cause is what's right." Blasphemous as it may sound, they may find that their employees or the community may come first. Let me put it this way: If you have just enough change in your pocket to make that eleventh hour phone call to save your business and keep your cause alive, who would you call? Or, to put it in less extreme context, if you have just enough money to print one brochure that tells what your business does and why it does it, who do you want to make sure, first and foremost, the writing and design of the brochure is directed to?

What Stops You from Telling the Truth?

What is your competitive climate? What are the emotional, psychological, political, and economic obstacles blocking your path? These questions shouldn't surprise anyone who has had to construct a marketing plan. Competitive analysis is often a good chunk of such a plan, sometimes as much as 50 percent of a three-inch, three-ring binder. For the purposes of creating a realistic communications strategy, you should answer this question with complete realism. Call out other businesses or organizations that are, or could be, competitors. Call out any other issues that may be standing in the way of you achieving your cause.

These issues may be psychological obstacles. They can be emotional roadblocks. They can be driven by economics. They can be internal obstacles within your organization, such as cultural or operational issues. These obstacles can be readily evident, big, and sometimes monstrous. They can also be hidden landmines or stealth-like forces waiting beneath the radar. Whatever they are, make sure you take note of them. The answer to this question is a true reality check for your business. If there is one guiding principle in cause-based communications, it is the realization that the best way to deal with your competitive climate is to know who and what it is and to deal and speak to it with absolute truth and integrity. This is an area of communications planning where fear loves to feed. You are going to look that fear right in the eye and master it.

I want you to take the classic economic meaning of competition and wrestle with it in terms of how your business and organization can achieve its cause. Most see competition as a pillar of capitalism that fuels innovation, efficiency, and low prices. Microeconomic theory believes that pure competition is the most efficient means of allocating resources. It makes businesses create new products and services that provide the customer with more selection and improved products. More selection usually leads to lower prices, as opposed to pricing situations under a monopoly or oligopoly.

Ask yourself and your team what you are competing for? Is it profit? Are you hoping to defeat something? Is it something bad? Is it good? What is the size of the competition? Are you a business competing locally or a corporate giant dueling for global market share, talent, and resources? What are the consequences of your competition? Is it casual? Is it for fun? Is it for pride? Or is it a bitter rivalry? Is it like a war? How does this bump up against the idea of your business as a cause? Is your cause feeling like a noble cause? What damage needs to occur for you to achieve your cause? Who will suffer? Who will gain?

Inter-species competition can be seen as the shaping influence around adaptation and evolution. Social Darwinists believe competition can help determine who and what is best politically, economically, and environmentally. Do you feel your cause separates the strong from the weak? Are the obstacles standing in the way of people and things that are superior or inferior to your cause? How do you feel when your cause is placed in a hierarchy of importance?

It doesn't take a Nobel Prize in economics to know that competition can have a less than positive impact upon both humans and the planet. Negative effects range from damaging other living things to the depletion of valuable resources and energy supplies. Competition often demands enormous financial reserves. Competition can soften ethical principles to gain the upper hand. Competition can hurt the team because it pushes itself beyond its limits to win, therefore losing. Ironically, going full throttle for competitive advantage can actually hurt company profitability.

Throughout history, philosophers' attention to competition is almost always as a footnote, giving its due as being part of our society and by noting the positive and negative aspects of it in political and economic settings. There doesn't seem to be much philosophical energy or discourse around the core nature of competition and its impact on ethics. Some minds have seen competition as being the enemy of cooperation, while others see competition and cooperation as necessary roommates. These philosophers see healthy competition demanding cooperation, respect and honoring of rulings by unbiased judges, and the agreement on spoils from the competition.

Is competition moral? Who benefits from competition? Who suffers? Is the suffering justified? Are the benefits hoarded or shared, revealed or hidden, financial or spiritual? Can they be both? Does the competition call for only one winner? What happens to the losers? What happens to the winner? Why is it set up as a game to begin with? What comes to mind when you hear the term "cola wars"? What comes to mind when you hear "war games"? Think about the meaning of these terms in the context of your business or organization: contestant, champion, comer, finalist, foe, front-runner, favorite, world-beater, king, leader, number one.

Take an inventory of your collaborative climate. What joint operations, actions, or cooperation are essential for the success of your cause? What are the forces working with you? What can you create rather than destroy?

"Fully integrated" individuals and leaders realize that they must work with both their personal strengths and weaknesses. Functional families realize they must work together for the betterment of each family member, which results in the overall health of the family. Healthy corporate cultures rely on true collaboration among departments and teams and offices rather than a divisive "winners and losers" approach to the bottom line. A collaboration-based profit and loss statement is stronger than one built by a winner-take-all, master-of-the-universe mentality. Think about this when you construct your collaborative climate. Compare your competitive and collaborative analysis. See which one feels most aligned with your cause. Think about what the difference is between being better than others and doing better *for* others.

What Is Your Collaborative Climate?

Take a 360-degree view of your organization. Look at it from both the inside out and outside in. See yourself as others see you. Create an inventory of your weaknesses and the strengths of the competition. Think in terms of both physical competition and philosophical roadblocks. When you feel you have created a comprehensive competitive overview, select the number one obstacle standing in the way of your success.

Conduct a review of your collaborative climate. Again, look at what's being done internally or what could be done in terms of collaboration. How do others regard you from the perspective of collaboration? What is your most effective means of working with others? What is stopping you from collaborating with others? What would happen if you pursued a collaborative relationship with your main competitor? Or, with any competitor? What would happen if you worked with the attitudinal, economical, and environmental obstacles standing in your way rather than always going against them?

Compare your competitive analysis with your collaborative review. Which one most connects and supports your business cause?

What's Truly in It for Them?

What is the key benefit you provide to your audience? The answer to this question forces you to truly move from cause to effect. Your business cause will be something quite meaningful to your organization, but it may not benefit your key audiences. You must be able to truthfully translate your primary benefit into a principal idea that will then underline all communications. This is your marketing value proposition. This is your benefit statement. This is the part of your story that serves the interests of your key audiences. It's the answer to "what's in it for me?"

For example, a research foundation's cause or reason for existence is to "ensure your discoveries improve the human condition." But what about its audience or its primary customer—CEOs of technology companies? What direct benefit can they get from the research foundation's improvement of the human condition? The answer is very specific to the needs of its primary audience. "We have over 1,500 fresh technologies that can improve your bottom line."

Another example is the bank reviewed in Chapter Three. The bank exists to "personally help," but what's in it for "me," its primary audience? The answer is that the bank "will personally help you achieve financial health and freedom."

Sometimes your cause is embedded or integrated into your benefit statement. Sometimes it isn't. An effective benefit statement needs to be truthful and authentic. What makes your benefit statement different from your cause is that your benefit statement is unique to you. It is something you can own. It is something only you can legitimately promise to your market. For example, your cause could be to "alleviate poverty." Chances are there will be other businesses or organizations that have this as their cause. But chances are they are in different industries or different markets. And, if they are in a similar industry as you, you most likely are helping to alleviate poverty in a way they aren't. The answer to this question should appeal to either the self-interest of your audience or their market-interest. It's what you do, what you provide, what you offer that is of direct benefit to them.

Let's take a minute and discuss the difference between features and benefits. Benefits are the good things that happen to your customers or primary audience when they use or are involved in your business, product, or its services. Although we are focusing on your primary benefit, it is important for you to know how best to express the features of your product or service. Clarity here is just as important as in any other aspect of communications. You may find that your features are part of the support points you'll be collecting in the next chapter. A features list for your product, service, and business is best communicated where space allows you to go into more detail and description. Features of a shoe may include what the sole is made of, how pointed the toe is, the arch architecture, color choices, and whether it comes with a guarantee.

Your value proposition or your primary benefit is shaped by the benefits of using your product or service. The most effective marketing always focuses on a single most important benefit. Your benefit emerges from the experience of using your product or service. When you consider benefits, consider the question, "What does my primary audience receive from experiencing this feature?"

To go back to the shoe example, what is the benefit of your shoe having a slip-proof sole? What are the benefits of its arch architecture replicating the arches of Olympic runners? What are the benefits of the shoe being available in purple?

Classic benefit statements usually talk about how convenient you make things, or how you save time and money, or how much experience you have. Take a look at car marketing. Brochures for cars may list features, but their core impression with their audience is based on benefit. Car buyers are not determining what to purchase based on the steering radius or the tire pressure or the number of cup holders. They buy the car because of how it will impact their life in general. How will they feel in the car? How will others feel in their car? Will their children be happy in the car? This is an emotional appeal. It touches what people think of themselves and makes the car part of that definition or perception. Now, imagine if you take this classic Madison Avenue thinking and integrate the aspect of *cause* into it. Suddenly emotions become real and perception is stripped of the superficial.

Now, look at your features. Pick the most significant feature in terms of providing audience benefit. Will that feature save time and money? Will it cure a disease? Will it make them more comfortable? Will it improve their relationships with others? With themselves? Will it help them achieve things they have always dreamed of achieving or doing? Will it make their world a better place?

You are not writing a tagline or headline here. You are crafting the most crystal clear and focused value proposition possible. This statement will be the kernel or nugget from which taglines, headlines, ads, and other communication tools emerge. There is no pressure to create a statement that is poetic or clever or entertaining or shocking. The key is to use laser-like precision in explaining what you have to offer your audience that makes them want to learn more or make contact with you.

One sentence captures and communicates the key value that you bring to the marketplace. That value is always being framed around the hopes and aspirations of your key audience. But here is where the real power of communicating from a place of cause lives. It compels you to elevate your value to a place that fulfills meaningful wants and needs. Once you have discovered and validated your noble business cause, it will be virtually impossible for you to go the route of dumbing-down, spinning, hyping, or manipulating the marketplace. You will naturally appeal to the higher instincts, intentions, and dreams of your audiences. This is also where you realize that this approach to business and communications is the courageous breath of fresh air you have been waiting for.

Always keep in mind that your benefit statement is a means to an end. It is your means of attracting and keeping customers or supporters. It's this relationship between you and your customer that determines how well you will achieve your cause. It's the cause of your business that drives your need to connect to the marketplace. It's the cause of your business that transforms typical "brand promises" into benefits that truly make things better. Just as your cause creates deep meaning and passion for you and your business, your benefit statement will have the meaning necessary to create passionate loyalty and buy-in from your customers and audiences. Your benefit statement should have great redeeming value as opposed to creating redeeming value via coupons and rebates.

What Is Your Primary Benefit?

Consider what it is that you do that makes someone want to do business with you. What do you do that causes them to stop, consider, buy, invest, support, partner, or learn more about you? What is the value proposition you have for your audience? What do you have to offer them that will make things better for them, or help them meet an important need? What makes this benefit unique to your business? What makes this benefit truly compelling? Craft a short and sweet statement that captures this benefit. Is it true? Is it meaningful? Does it fortify the fulfillment of your cause? Make sure every word in this statement counts.

Be True to Your Word

What single word best captures your benefit and message? Before you commit to your word, you also have to abide by this rule: the word must be present in your primary benefit statement.

This is the question where the poet in an organization can get a bit fulfilled. The idea of boiling down your value proposition to just one word displays an appreciation of the power and significance of words usually absent in the language of business. Look at your benefit statement and from it choose the word that best captures your proposition. The selection of your key word will drive the form, content, character, and creativity of your communications. This word will become the fulcrum point for your story.

This is the question where the planning team around the table is pulled in two directions. The first is the desire to achieve something they have really never done before, i.e., capture the essence of their message in one word. The other is the notion that capturing what they are all about with one word isn't possible, that a complex, multifaceted, diverse organization can't be defined so simply. It's this tension that galvanizes thinking on the part of the team. That results not only in the business finding its word but also the team finding itself on the same page.

The determination of a key word sets in motion the development of incredibly focused and innovative communication solutions. You may think that narrowing it all down to one single word is stifling, limiting, and will shackle the imagination. Quite the opposite occurs. This precise selection of one word is actually liberating. It structures the frame for creating communications, but not the creative itself. All too often communication concepts are created in a void and end up being communications for communications sake. Or, they emerge from such a thick, complex brief that the big idea looks thick and complex. The absolute clarity and focus provided by your key word results in crystal-clear, grounded but still highly creative conceptual solutions.

Bear in mind, the actual word you select is not necessarily going to be in your tagline, headlines, copy and every piece of messaging you create. But, it might. More often, the intent and meaning of the word will be present in your communications. If you choose *elegant* as your key word, it's not a given that the word elegant would ever be present in your communication materials. But the meaning of elegant would be present in your materials. Or, if you choose the word *responsible* as your key word, you may well determine that it should literally be present in your story, no matter where or how it is being told.

The word you pick will indeed make all the difference in the emotional and intellectual qualities of your message. Think of how you react to "Living the American Dream" versus "Living the American Future." The response to the word dream is quite a bit different than the word future. Taking the dream theme further, imagine if Dr. King announced, "I have a strategic goal" instead of "I have a dream." It takes you to a totally different place, doesn't it?

Choosing your key word is where you will sow the seeds of success or failure. Your word choice will change meaningless meanderings into a powerfully steady statement. Consider the weight or intent of your word as well. Don't hedge your words. What a difference it makes to say "I should," or "I ought to," versus "I will."

Make sure your word stays true to the meaning of the word. Words have connotative and denotative meanings. The denotative meaning is the dictionary meaning, the one that we all refer to when trying to learn or understand language. For example, take the word car. Its denotative meaning is a road vehicle, usually with four wheels and powered by an internal-combustion engine, designed to carry a small number of passengers. Then there is the connotative definition. This is the meaning each of us has in our heads and attaches to the word upon hearing or reading it. Someone who hears the word car most likely will see his perception of a car. It could be a Porsche or a Kia or a Lincoln Town Car or an SUV or hybrid. It could represent where a first kiss took place or it could conjure up a tragic moment. The reaction is not common to all, but a perception and realization based on the individual's context. To add clarity, we begin to add adjectives and adverbs: fast car, cool car, sexy car, functional car, or economical car.

The significance of the connotative meaning of a word is its powerful emotional content. Your primary audience will react emotionally rather than intellectually when they encounter the word. Look at the word mouse. Its traditional denotative meaning is a small rodent found all over the world that has a brown or grayish-brown coat and a long mostly hairless tail. Not very emotional or engaging. Now think of Mickey Mouse, Jerry Mouse, Pinky and the Brain, Speedy Gonzalez, Stuart Little, The Three Blind Mice, The City Mouse and the Country Mouse, and *Of Mice and Men*. All can be vivid and emotional and connotative expressions of mice that go way beyond the denotative meaning.

The greatest impact of words comes from using the connotative meanings to affect an audience's emotional response. One reason for this is that you cannot debate, argue with, or mathematically dissect emotions because they don't live in the world of logic. Embrace and employ your word this way and your audience will align with you at an emotional level, which will strengthen your intellectual relationship with them as well. The key is to make the emotional connection true and authentic. Capture it in the truest sense of the word.

Emotions aside, words play an undeniable role in our world. When was the last time you Googled? Or did a word search? Relationships, knowledge, and commerce all are being shaped, formed, and fueled, often by one word. Frank Outlaw wrote: " Watch your thoughts; they become your words. Watch your words; they become your actions. Watch your actions; they become your habits. Watch your habits; they become your character. Watch your character for it will become your destiny."

With this inspiration, begin the process of determining your key word. Begin by reviewing your benefit statement, your final answer to the previous question. What you have crafted there serves up what you have available as a key word. Remember, your key word must be embedded somewhere in that statement. To show how this works, here is a working example. Consider the benefit statement:

We can personally help you achieve financial health and freedom.
There are ten words to choose from for the key word:

1. We
2. Can
3. Personally
4. Help
5. You
6. Achieve
7. Financial
8. Health
9. And
10. Freedom

What a world of difference it will make if you choose the word *freedom* instead of any of the others. Or *personally*, instead of *financial*. The selection of any one of these words will take your communications down a very distinct path. That path will be entirely devoted to communicating your complete benefit statement, but the view from the path will be impacted by the key word. In this example, the bank chose the word "personally." The meaning of the word personally runs throughout all its communications and operations. Although the word itself isn't present in the bank's tagline, its meaning is loud and clear.

Go back and take a look at your benefit statement. Make sure it's the one you want to go with. Then be extremely deliberative in choosing your key word. Write down why you chose that one word over the others. Write a working definition of that word based on your business and your cause. Develop a connotative and denotative definition of your word. Get a feel for the emotional impact of the word. Does the word require an adjective or adverb to make it work better? Why? Are you excited about your word? Did you find yourself going back and rewriting your benefit statement so you could have different words to choose from? Why did that happen? Did the word you choose surprise you? Is the word also in your cause?

A Matter of Facts

You've created your benefit statement. This is your promise to your audience. It's that special thing only you can do for them. Whatever your promise, it needs to be believed. No matter how inspiring your proposition is, it must be soaked in truth and validation. Why should people believe you? Why should your primary benefit be trusted? What are the support points and facts that validate your proposition? These are your reasons to believe. They are the facts that make your value proposition believable. If you tell your audience, "We are the best at what we do," that just won't cut it. You need to get specific as to why you are the best. Real facts. Real figures. Real examples. Data. Testimonials. Success stories. The proof.

Feel free to go back to your review of features and benefits. Many of your features will find a home in your list of reasons to believe. What you need to do is translate each and every one of your features into a benefit. If a car is "guaranteed to go without breakdown for five years," the company needs to let its audience know why that's a good thing for them. You may be so close to your features that you obviously know the benefits. But it may not be so obvious to your primary audience. Your reasons to believe will actually be a compilation of other benefit statements, all pledging allegiance to your primary benefit.

Your promise may have just one or two support points. For example, you may make the claim, "This hybrid car not only gets 65 mpg, but also seats seven." Your support point is the official, sealed miles-per-gallon rating report and the actual seat count inside the car. However, if you claim, "This hybrid car is the most comfortable hybrid car on the market," you need to go deeper with your reasons to believe. You may have to see if there are actual "comfort meters" or "comfort indexes" that you can refer to. You may have to get hundreds of testimonials from owners who swear this car is the most comfortable. You may have to list, outline, and explain all the features and benefits of the car that help make it comfortable. Let those benefits support your claim and let your customer then determine if that all adds up to the most comfort.

Some of the businesses I have worked with have one, incredibly powerful fact that drives their promise into the receptive hearts and minds of their audience. Other businesses and organizations have pages upon pages of support points. When there is so much validation, it's always good to prioritize. Give your top five reasons to believe. The key is to be as efficient as possible in sharing the facts. If your customer wants to know more, then go deeper with the facts and figures. Sometimes, the nature of a product or service or idea requires complex validations in order to earn trust. This is fine if your audience has that kind of attention span and time to devote to your proposition. But often it doesn't. My suggestion is that, ideally, you should be able to state your promise and present memorable powerful reasons to believe in 200 words or less, about a two-minute presentation. And for those short elevator rides or fast-moving network events, write a version of your benefit statement that's no more than 100 words.

Cause for Action

You've made your promise. You've made your case. You've earned trust. Your audience believes in you. Now, what do you want them to do? This question is deceptively simple. The first reaction is, well, buy my product. Or hire my services. Or, support my idea. But, unless you have a contract in hand and your customer across the table, how do you prompt the kind of action that will lead to gaining and retaining them as a customer or supporter? You can have a beautifully designed brochure, an exquisitely produced TV spot, and an irresistible direct mail piece, but there's no clear call to action. The recipient has to guess what you want him to do. You can't assume that your customers will know why they should act, how they should act, or when they must act.

Take a look at the vast number of late night infomercials. They work. They pound away at the viewer to call a toll-free number with a credit card in hand. And if you call right now, they'll also provide you with a free gift with your purchase, but only if you act immediately. This formula works. And it can work for you, even if you are in the most elegant of message settings, whether you are communicating on the web, over the airwaves, in a print ad, or at a fundraising luncheon. Your call to action can be remarkably easy, such as "order today." Or it could be an ongoing step-by step process. If your intent is to sell something, try to skip the "call for more information" and directly ask your audience to purchase your product, enlist your services, or support your initiative.

Let your primary audience know when and how to contact you. Unless you're involved in a unique or time-sensitive marketing endeavor, it's best to create a sense of immediacy. Customers forget quickly, so the sooner you can get them to respond, the better. Traditionally, call-to-actions come at the end of a marketing message. Put your call to action throughout your story. Do it with the passion you unearthed when you captured your cause. Your cause-based call to action must be sincere, genuine, and from the heart.

An effective call to action can change results sometimes 20 to 30 percent. Make sure your call to action is sensitive and respectful of where your audience currently is in your relationship with them. This could mean that your call to action is evolutionary. Are your customers learning more about a problem? Experiencing a demonstration? Studying data? Presented with a time-sensitive offer? Is your call action-oriented? Does it ask, "learn how" or "learn now"?

Here are some examples of often-applied calls to action:

Call (number) to learn more.

Call (number of specific person) and speak to (actual name) to learn more.

Call to make an appointment.

Call for a free consultation.

Call for our free brochure.

Call for our free video/DVD.

Call toll free and order now.

Call toll free and order now and save ($).

Call toll free, order now and get (premium).

Visit our website to learn more.

Visit our website and download a free brochure.

Visit our website and click "free" for your special gift.

Visit our website to learn about our trial offer.

Redeem this coupon.

Visit our showroom.

Make reservations tonight.

Make a donation by writing to:

To volunteer, call:

For a free kit, call or write or visit our website.

You get the message. There are myriad ways to prompt action from your audience. Sometimes it can be very specific and price or time sensitive, other times very general and philosophical/values based.

What Is Your Call to Action?

Look at your business. Look at your cause. Review your competitive climate. Get to know your primary audience and other audiences as well as possible. Look at your promise to that audience. Look at how you have earned their trust and belief in that promise. Based on these observations, what is the ideal next step you want your audience to perform? Is it simply a matter of visiting your website to learn more about you? Or are you in a place where you are asking for the sale or donation? How do you make that happen in the most pain-free way for your audience? How do you make that happen so that you begin to build a long-lasting relationship with that audience? What's your call to action? Is it one easy step? Or is this the first step in a long courtship? Make sure your call to action reflects the values of your business. And make sure it is something you can deliver and fulfill.

Your True Voice

This is the question where you really need to know thyself. Imagine your business or organization is a person. That person (your business) has a personality and character traits. If you don't believe this, stop for a moment and picture in your mind American Airlines and what kind of image appears. Now picture Virgin Airlines. Both are airlines, but have completely different personalities. What do you see and feel when you picture IBM? Now think of Apple Computers. Both are computer companies, but there is a big difference in personalities. The personality of your business is a critical question that helps you transcend old school thinking that every business or organization is merely what shows on the ledger sheet.

Imagine if that person (your business) were to walk into a room. What would he or she look like? Is your business a "he" with a male voice or a "she" with a female voice? What is your business wearing? Subdued grays? Pastels? Earth tones or vibrant colors? Are you formal or casual? How old are you? Are you a listener? Or do you lead the conversation? Are you more verbal or more visual? What kind of car, if any, does your business drive? What is your favorite sport or entertainment? Favorite music? Books? Magazines? Political leanings? Is your business single? Married? Kids? Do you live in the city? Country? What is your greatest fear in life? What brings you the greatest joy? Is your business always very serious? Funny? Are you the strong, silent type, or the life of the party? Although all this may sound a bit soul-bearing for a business, it is incredibly important. What you are doing is giving your business a human framework. This is necessary when driving your business from a cause-based foundation. With cause comes passion. With passion comes humanity. With humanity comes the place where business strips away the veneer of quiet desperation and the protective, suffocating armor it has worn for far too long. A business that performs from a place of cause and purpose must engage the marketplace as a living, breathing person, not as a financial statement. To trust you and do business with you, your audience needs to know who you are. Therefore, you need to know who you are.

This is an exercise in realizing who you really are and feeling comfortable in that skin. This is about your business capturing its authentic personality. This is not about building a brand, but building character. This is about making sure your story is told the only way it can be told. Answer this question the way it should be answered and you will find the voice of your marketing and communications to be more confident, charismatic, and welcomed by your marketplace.

Some of the relationship-based "types" embraced by Madison Avenue include:

- **The down-to-earth, family oriented, genuine, old-fashioned type.** This they call "sincerity." Sincerity brands are Hallmark, Kodak, and sometimes Coca-Cola. The relationship is akin to one that resides with a well-liked and respected member of the family.

- **The spirited, young, up-to-date outgoing type.** Pepsi goes after this type. This relationship would be spending a weekend night with a friend who is young and spirited.

- **The accomplished, influential, competent type.** Hewlett-Packard and *The Wall Street Journal* are this type. This relationship is one you would have with a person you respect for what he has achieved. Business computer marketing often strives for this relationship with their customers.

- **The pretentious, wealthy, condescending type.** BMW, Mercedes, Lexus fit this mold. This relationship is like the one you would have with a powerful CEO or wealthy relative.

- **The athletic and outdoorsy type.** Nike, Marlboro and Wells Fargo fit in here. This relationship is one you would have when coordinating an outing with a good friend who loves the outdoors.

These "types" are just a sampling of the matrixes, models, methodologies and magic that traditional brand builders bring to the causeless brand party. Stay away from this stuff, no matter how tempting it may be. The power of your cause is that it transcends types and models. Your personality is your personality.

What Is Your Voice?

Begin now to visualize your business or organization as a person. Describe that person in as much detail as possible. Create a personality study of your business. Capture its strengths in personality as well as its weaknesses. Begin by asking yourself, if your business walked into the room, would it appear as a male or female? Answering this key question no doubt will set the stage for how you continue to profile the human aspects of your business. Then begin to shape that complete person. Be as literal or cerebral as you need to be. Describe your organization's day from the moment it gets out of bed to when it puts its head on the pillow at the end of the day. This process can begin to describe everything. Do you wake up to an alarm or naturally? If it is an alarm—is it music, a beep, or a Zen gong? What do you have for breakfast? Do you even have breakfast? You can have fun with this. But make sure the fun always reflects the cause of your business.

True to Form

Here we are, at the finish line, and there is good reason for this being the final question. This is last because it usually is first. Clients often approach us and the first thing they say is, "We need a new brochure." Or they want a new logo. Or they say, "We need a campaign that addresses this issue." What they are asking for is a *tactic*. Brochures, websites, logos, ads, newsletters, TV and radio commercials are all tactical tools that work in service of the communications strategy or plan.

After you have completed your Mission in a Message, you may discover that the tool you thought you needed the most is something you really don't need at all. Or you may find out that you do need a new brochure, but the proposition and purpose of it has changed significantly.

What you need to do at this point is review your Mission-in-a-Message strategy. Really study it. Then determine, based on what you have created, what you need most to tell your story. What communication tools do you immediately need in hand to speak to your primary audience? What tools do you need to speak to your secondary audiences? Then, consider what tools you will need in the future.

Do you need a brochure or a multi-media campaign? Is it best to reach your audience via print or electronically? Are you talking local, grassroots, national, or international? What about the tools you need to communicate internally? What about budget? Is it unlimited? Are you going to re-do all your current materials at once? Or will the development of materials evolve over time? How segmented will your communications be?

Right now, don't worry about the actual creative. Concern yourself with the tactics, the format of those tactics, and whether they are the correct vehicles for making effective and efficient contact with your audience. The creative and content will be developed once your list of tools is outlined.

For example, Home Savings Bank, highlighted in Chapter Three, captured its cause and strategy with a new tagline, brochure, letterhead and business cards, website, product and service brochures, folders, newsletters, internal communications, newspaper and magazine ads, lobby graphics and shareholder materials. The arts advocacy organization highlighted in Chapter Four developed new letterhead and business cards, website, print ad campaign, electronic campaign, electronic newsletter, membership mailer, brochure, web banners, TV and radio public service announcements, cause-marketing materials, membership items, annual report, and an arts and business handbook.

What tools do you need to tell your story? Here's a checklist to get started:

1. New name
2. Logo & stationary package
3. Capabilities brochure
4. Specific products/Services brochures
5. Ads – *newspaper*
6. Ads – *magazine*
7. Direct mail – *print*
8. Direct mail – *electronic*
9. Outdoor/Transit
10. Posters
11. Presentation/Proposals materials
12. Website
13. Web banner ads

14. Chat rooms and blogs
15. Exhibits/Displays
16. Television
17. Radio
18. Packaging
19. Environmental/Signage
20. Yard signs
21. Doorhangers
22. Podcasts
23. CD-ROMs
24. Films and video
25. Internal messaging
26. Books
27. Workshops/Seminars
28. Press conferences
29. Roundtables
30. Cross-promotions
31. Product placements
32. Sponsorships
33. Events
34. Annual Reports
35. PowerPoint slides
36. Premiums
37. Press materials
38. Research
39. Product tags
40. Product sheets

You can't do it all, or can you? I've found it is often best to take an evolutionary approach to developing your communications tool chest.

If you need a new name, begin there and take as long as you need to get it right. Then roll out your name systematically, doing internal marketing and communications with your employees and investors or supporters first, then an external launch that will make the most effective appeal to your primary audience. If you have thirty brochures that need to be redone with the new name and identity, and you can't do them all at once, prioritize and roll out on an as-needed basis.

If you need six months to a year to build a new website based on your cause-based position and voice, create a placeholder page in the meantime that provides a snapshot of who and what you do and why you are doing it.

When all is said and done, your tools and materials should work in harmony, capitalize on economies of scale, and always stay true to the voice and cause. You may need to update fonts and photos and outdated terms, but you should always be confident that the message is enduring and doesn't need to be changed, but bolstered and enhanced over time.

EIGHT

Good For You

CONGRATULATIONS! You have just completed your Mission in a Message. Sit back. Take a look at it. What do you see? Do you see a roadmap for communicating in a way that will benefit not only your company, but also every one it makes contact with? Do you see a blueprint for success, the kind of success that stands the tests of time? Do you see a communications plan that is more than a communications plan? Do you see a document that can help guide both day-to-day and long-term business planning and decision-making? If you and your leadership team have rolled up your sleeves and answered Questions 1 through 10 the way they should be answered, you now have in your hands a communications plan that is written from a strong, enduring place of purpose, that doesn't shortchange the power of passion, and realizes that a combination of purpose and passion leads to the kind of success from which everyone profits.

Championing Your Cause: Taking It Personally

A good chunk of the underlying proposition of this book is making sure your personal values and beliefs don't get hung up at the coat rack when you go to work, but instead they are honored, respected, and can actually thrive. To make sure you, personally, are on the same page as your business, how about working on your personal Mission in a Message? This exercise will not only help reveal how your personal values, principles, and beliefs are aligned with what you do for a living and where you do it, it will also provide you with a blueprint for how you can tell your own story most effectively. We all have a story to tell. Having a personal Mission in a Message in hand might be what you need to get a clearer picture of what is important to you, what you are passionate about, and how best to let the world know. So, when you're ready, take some time and go through these ten questions. Are you ready to begin integrating *your* personal and professional cause? Ready to realize the *why* of what *you* do? Ready to find *your* own true north? Champion your own cause. It's time to take it personally.

> *Never apologize for showing feeling.*
> *When you do so, you apologize for truth.*
>
> Benjamin Disraeli

_____

(Your Name)

My Mission in a Message
Communicating My Cause

1 My True Cause
"Why" do I do "what" I do? Why do I exist? What would the world and my community be like if I didn't exist or were to leave?

_____

_____

_____

2 Why Tell My Truth?
What will communicating my cause accomplish for me? For others? (Noble, enduring, this is not about blowing my horn. It's about telling my story.)

_____

_____

_____

3 Tell "Them" the Truth
Who are my audiences? Who is my primary audience? What do I know about them? What do they know about me?

_____

_____

_____

4 What's Stopping Me from Telling the Truth
What is the competitive climate? What is being said by others? What are the emotional, psychological, political and economic obstacles in my way?

_____

_____

_____

5 What's Truly In It for Them
What is the key benefit I can provide to my key audience? My value proposition? What is the principal idea that underlies all my communication?

_____

_____

_____

6 True to My Word

What single word captures my benefit and primary idea? Yes, one word!
(This word needs to be present in my value proposition, my answer to
Question Five.)

_____

7 A Matter of Facts

Why should people believe me? What are the support points and facts that validate my proposition? Why should my primary benefit and promise be trusted?

_____

_____

_____

8 Cause for Action

What is the desired action? What do I want my audience to do? What am I
trying to achieve when they hear my story?

_____

_____

_____

9 Your True Voice

What is the character and personality of my cause? My true colors? What does
my cause look, taste, smell, feel and sound like? What's my style, my tone?

_____

_____

_____

10 True to Form

What things, tools, aids, etc. do I need to tell my story?

_____

_____

_____

Appendix

Cause for Celebration

IF YOU ARE WONDERING how your Mission in a Message looks in relationship to others, we offer several condensed samples for you to review. We emphasize the word condensed! All the deep discussion about cause, all the debate about audiences, all the vibrant conversation about key benefits and the key word have been edited. What the examples reveal are the short and sweet answers to each question. Even though they are shortened, they will serve as helpful, snapshot-like benchmarks for you. Make sure you find an appropriate way to keep a record of your discussion and analysis. It will be of immense value when it comes to creating and crafting your story. The examples cover a range of businesses and organizations. These Mission in a Message snapshots will help you in shaping and molding your Mission in a Message, not in terms of duplicating them, but in realizing just how unique you can be in the creation of your plan.

Health Care Cooperative

1 Our True Cause

To create premium care at the most affordable price.

2 Why Tell Our Truth?

Raised awareness of who we are will strengthen our ability to fulfill our mission: unifying and leading member employers in the pursuit of a value-based, market-driven health care system. This will allow us to provide real choice, resulting in premier care at the most affordable price.

3 Tell "Me" the Truth

CEOs of regional businesses employing at least 150.

4 What's Stopping Us from Telling the Truth

Other HMOs. Other networks. Other coalitions. National carriers. Traditional carriers. Agents. The attitude that choice results in higher costs. The resistance to "complicating things."

5 What's Truly in It for Them

We provide real choice resulting in a plan that is your plan—a plan that delivers top quality care at the most affordable cost.

6 True to My Word

Choice

7 A Matter of Facts

Ninety-eight percent of the area's providers are part of our network. We provide employers and employees objective information enabling their best choice. We are data rich and have unmatched expertise in our field. We are a non-profit—which translates to objectivity. We offer system-wide quality improvement. 34 different administrators punctuate the flexibility of our plans. Our access to hundreds of providers results in savings on everything from drugs to dental. Our preferred pricing and added value results in choice that doesn't cost more. We are completely transparent. Members are owners. In essence, you own us, we work for you.

8 Cause for Action

Contact the Alliance to learn more about how we can help.

9 Our True Voice

Our voice is dramatic. Passionate, mission driven. Honesty, integrity, "the higher ground." Spirit and energy of an advocate. Irreverent. Unexpected. Transparent.

10 True to Form

We are developing a campaign. The initial business-to-business phase will utilize appropriate media to reach our target audience. Tactics can include ads in business publications, direct mail, possibly outdoor events and member partnership messaging.

Hotel

1 Our True Cause

To create a sense of community, both internally and externally.

2 Why Tell Our Truth?

If we didn't share this story it would just be business as usual.

3 Tell "Me" the Truth

Local community member with skew of male, upper income, and our secondary audience is the internet community.

4 What's Stopping Us from Telling the Truth

Local downtown hotels. Chain hotels. Hilton. Suburban hotels. Our biggest challenge is that most hotels are newer and can provide things in their rooms we don't right now. Burb hotels—cheaper, can use car, easy in and out, new. For restaurants—traffic and parking can be a barrier. The economy.

5 What's Truly in It for Them

Our hotel is the best way to connect to the community.

6 True to My Word

Community

7 A Matter of Facts

We are the biggest and most acclaimed hotel in the city. We're located right in the heart of downtown. You can walk to the Capitol, the city's most famous and fantastic shopping district, theatre and arts districts, restaurants, world-class university, parks and lakes. Inside you also find a community that's easy to connect with. Featuring superior guest services, concierge and a can-do attitude. Our 5-star service is warm, personal and real. We aren't franchised or corporate—people can truly make a difference here. You'll enjoy beautiful guest rooms, award-winning restaurants, pool, sauna, fitness center, meeting and banquet rooms, vibrant jazz bar with live music. We're a hotel in love with our city and support all kinds of events and activities that help to make it the special place it is—from the arts to sports to social issues. When you walk into our lobby, you'll immediately feel a connection with the hotel and the city. Anybody can build rooms, not everyone can be this committed to the community.

8 Cause for Action

Book a room(s) and/or meeting, recommend hotel to others.

9 Our True Voice

Our voice is that of a warm, gracious host. We are wise and experienced. There is depth in our voice. Our roots run deep. We are articulate, cultured, prestigious but not pretentious. We are a melting pot with customer and employee diversity. We are cerebral. Smart. Entertaining. Humorous. Our current ads and collateral capture this voice in many respects.

10 True to Form

We will create a campaign that captures our strategy. It will be evolutionary and as each particular communication tool comes up for renewal, it will embrace this strategy. We will continue with our copy approach but frame things a bit differently (commitment to community). Key components include: rack brochure, meeting planner brochure, Governor's Club brochure, website, business cards/letterhead, newsletters, e-letters, posters, general print ads, event ads, restaurant ads, television, radio, banner ads, environmental graphics, in-hotel messaging, signage, direct mail, all other collateral.

Hospital

1 Our True Cause

To fulfill the honor to serve.

2 Why Tell Our Truth?

It is critical that everyone in this organization—physicians, employees, board members, volunteers—realizes that it is our honor to serve patients. Internally, if our people don't understand and believe this, there will be a disconnect. Likewise, if we don't tell our story to the community we won't be able to make the money we need to continue to fulfill our mission. We want to make sure the community knows the role we play and the void there would be if we didn't exist. Our cause could set the tone for individual behavior within the organization in regard to customer interaction. Making an honorable connection with people in the community will create an infinite loyalty. Telling our story will help. It will help in our relations with the Medical Foundation. We want the community to see us as an organization that they want to nurture. We want to get to that magical place where the community says, "Thank goodness they are here." It is important to tell our story both internally and externally. Our organization can't endure without doing this.

3 Tell "Me" the Truth

The community we serve (with a first subset being community leaders).

4 What's Stopping Us from Telling the Truth

Past history related to mergers and almost mergers. Perception that we're a big business. Sense of corporate medicine. Being a charity versus corporate medicine. Some perception of commercial enterprise—people don't know we're not for profit. Perception that we're a city hospital like

"St. Elsewhere." From a communications standpoint we struggle with community being a positive or a negative. Physicians' perceptions. Physician group competitors. Physicians feel conflicting loyalties. Lots of voices in community. Other hospitals—competitors both in delivery of health care and for charitable dollars. Our cause and message are more complex than the other two hospitals' (faith & research). We make our message so broad that we lose our ability to be the best. We can never achieve more than we see ourselves achieving. We have the second-most baby deliveries in the state—but who knows? Our name is an undefined term. We struggle with how to identify ourselves. Cost of health care. Health care costs are rising more and more to the surface—people are bringing this closer and closer to home. Broad public reimbursement system. Changing demographics of the area we serve.

5 What's Truly in It for Them

We make life better for everyone here.

6 True to My Word

Everyone

7 A Matter of Facts

By fulfilling our mission to heal this day, teach for tomorrow, embrace excellence always and serve our communities for a lifetime of quality care—we make life better for everyone here. For well over a century, sustaining the quality of life in this community has indelibly been a part of who we are. We collaborate and step forward to provide services that many people may not need, but without such services, the community would suffer. We provide quality care from the very beginnings of life to its final moments. From our prenatal program for low-income women, our birthing center and neonatal care unit to our heart center, extensive retirement services and our home health program enabling individuals to receive care in the comfort of their own homes—we make life better for everyone. We are home to the National Center of Excellence in Women's Health and the Cardiovascular Center of Excellence Heart Center. We serve more emergency patients than anyone else in the community. We have a committed, diverse and loyal workforce, with a record of longevity other hospitals envy. Today, gifts through our foundation provide the margin of excellence to ensure our commitment to making life better for everyone.

8 Cause for Action

Call, visit our website, or visit us in person to learn more about how we make life better for everyone here.

9 Our True Voice

We're primarily a female voice. We're not just going to tell you, we're going to show you. Sense of servitude and honor. Collaborative, caring and respectful. Humble and gracious. Professional but not formal. Intimate and personal. We are warm, approachable and authentic. Honest and sincere. We are serious but have a sense of lightness. We acknowledge our foibles and shortcomings. We are listeners—before you are heard you must listen. We are both verbal and visual. If we were a color, we would be blue. If we were a tree we would be an oak—deep roots, enduring, provide shelter and shade, go through the seasons of life. If we were a season, we would be spring—constantly searching for new beginnings, constant rebirth. If we were an animal, we'd be a St. Bernard—loyal, solid, dependable. If we were a car, we'd be a minivan—room for everyone. Enough creature comforts but nothing too fancy—a Chrysler Town & Country.

10 True to Form

This is an evolutionary campaign including logo/identity adjusting, positioning line, image advertising, product-line advertising, signage, brochures, foundation materials, employee materials, community outreach communication tools, and core tactical elements from television and radio to newspaper, billboard and magazine.

CPA Firm

1 Our True Cause

To create financially successful, caring and dynamic relationships that result in more than balancing the books.

2 Why Tell Our Truth?

To create financially successful, caring and dynamic relationships that result in more than balancing the books, we need to communicate on all levels. Relationships don't happen without communication.

3 Tell "Me" the Truth

Current clients.

4 What's Stopping Us from Telling the Truth

Other local and regional accounting firms and financial advisors—small to large. The Arthur Anderson/Enron phenomenon.

5 What's Truly in It for Them

A meaningful relationship resulting in more than balancing the books.

6 True to My Word

Relationship

7 A Matter of Facts

There's no question you will immediately realize we genuinely care about your business. We seek to understand you and your business. We build relationships with the people of the business, not just the business. We get personal in an impersonal world and understand the often-neglected emotional side of business. We achieve an authentic client chemistry that delivers continuous results. We always think "what's best for our clients." Our partners are key parts of the relationship with you, not mere acquaintances. We are along for the whole ride through the thick and the thin. We are part of your management team. We provide a full range of critical services that go beyond just accounting, even beyond the financial. We color outside the lines and provide "real" creative solutions. We provide expertise, working knowledge and innovative solutions for family businesses, hi-tech, construction and entrepreneurs. We believe maximizing wealth is a human journey. We know money can't buy you happiness—we know how to make money an effective down payment on happiness. We truly listen. We are trusted, locally grown, globally prepared and respect power, money, beauty and love. We maximize wealth through relationships based on heart, soul and brains.

8 Cause for Action

To continue to create financially successful, caring and dynamic relationships that result in more than balancing the books. Potential new clients will want to know more about us and call or visit our website to do so. Referral sources will have even more confidence referring us.

9 Our True Voice

Professional, friendly, witty. Not too stiff or too touchy-feely. Authentic and honest.

10 True to Form

Our story and messaging will work in all aspects of communications: ads, web, direct mail, brochures, radio, television, events, public relations, signage, sponsorships, workshop materials, electronic messaging, correspondence, product development, service pieces, proposal templates, internal materials.

Global Communications Company

1 Our True Cause

To create a better world through better communications.

2 Why Tell Our Truth?

By ensuring young people are heard, we will strengthen our mission of creating a better world through better communications—which will help us to be the most successful worldwide communications group. When we (adults) listen to young people and act on what we hear, we help ensure a more understanding and compassionate future.

3 Tell "Me" the Truth

Selecting the primary key audience segment from our audience universe, it would be our customers who support this initiative and come into daily contact with young people. Those customers most likely are parents and teachers. Identifying a prototypical person who reflects this key audience reveals a profile of "Mary," a 38-year-old teacher and parent of a 13-year-old girl and a 4-year-old boy who lives in the north part of a large metro area. She is married to a Post Office Manager. Joint income around £38K a year.

4 What's Stopping Us from Telling the Truth

If our audience, Mary, has obstacles in listening to young people at home or school it is because: there is not enough time; peer group pressure at school might discourage listening; she is tired; the 13-year-old is too embarrassed and prefers to talk to friends; some of what the 4-year-old talks about is seen to be relatively unimportant; she is a little complacent; she has always worked with kids and presumes she is really good (and she is pretty good).

5 What's Truly in It for Them

Listening is the answer.

6 True to My Word

Listening

7 A Matter of Facts

It's all been proven. Listening is the answer to ensuring young people are heard. Listening helps children grow up to show respect for their children. Listening saves you time. Listening lets you hear what makes your heart beat and opens your ears. Listening provides a great return on investment. Listening helps you explore new ideas and new worlds. Listening improves relationships, resolves issues and will make you feel good. Listening gives you time to hear what you want to hear. Listening helps you express yourself. Listening will answer all your questions. Listening will improve the lives of children, you, your family and your community.

8 Cause for Action

Listen

9 Our True Voice

The campaign's voice is the voice of our audience. When Mary or a teacher or employee or public official "listens," they should be inspired, uplifted and feel better about themselves and the world around them.

The voice of this campaign is honest, empathetic and "eye to eye." The voice of this campaign possesses all the virtues and traits of someone who listens to their self and others and realizes how they can in fact make things better. It is fluid, non-judgmental, inclusive and compassionate. By appealing to the individual voice the campaign will create a collective voice with immense power to make things better.

10 True to Form

We need all the tools necessary to be able to communicate with "Mary" at home, on the street and at school—for a sustained period of time.

Health Care Quality Improvement Organization

1 Our True Cause

Ensuring the healthiest lives possible.

2 Why Tell Our Truth?

We provide the tools and techniques that providers may not otherwise have access to for improving care; external tension for change, both by being there and by showing providers what other providers are doing—what's possible in terms of improvement; opportunity for collaboration—create connections between providers of health care so they can share best practices; partnership with independence—they don't have to worry about what our motives are, or how working with us will affect their competitiveness in the marketplace. We're in a situation where we need to reinforce that these things are still true—constantly create the value of working with us to providers. We do this to improve the care people get—and we can't do that directly ourselves, so we have to find the agents, and convince them to do the things we ask them to do. This requires constant communication. This organization communicates in order to have a relationship in order to make provisions happen. When marketing looks like propaganda or manipulation, it's a problem, but when it's from a place of truth—we can't do our work without it.

3 Tell "Me" the Truth

Providers

4 What's Stopping Us from Telling the Truth

Other QIOs—they can compete for our contracts, but often they seem more like partners than competitors. External resources—collaborations require the resources of those involved. Perception that the work with us won't yield an adequate ROI—quality isn't always something that can be reimbursed, it can be at times but sometimes it can cost even more. The entity that saves the money isn't necessarily the one doing the work. Prevention is not immediately apparent in cost-savings. Providers are being asked by different entities to do the same sorts of things—so they'll say no to us because they're already doing something similar—which can be a real or perceived duplication. Contracts are cyclical, and funding can change yearly. Turnover in staff (especially in nursing homes— huge turnover means constantly reintroducing us). Perception that we're a part of a regulatory apparatus by working with the government. Some of our work is following up on patient complaints, which can feel a little more like regulation. Economic barriers—with state contracts, our funding is an issue. But, overall, economics isn't a big factor because health issues aren't usually the first thing cut in the budget. Politics can have some impact on state contracts, but not necessarily with feds because it is longer-term. Awareness of us (there are large segments of the population, especially physicians, who we want to work with but who don't know who we are). Some baggage from the past—we're now kinder and gentler, but there is some memory of the past—up until 12 years ago our work was much more confrontational. Eight years ago, we changed our name. Now we're more educational, which was based on a study that said the old program was unnecessarily confrontational and wasn't doing anything to help patterns of care. The government took this study to heart and said, let's do it another way. The new name showed there was a new era, but there are still a few coattails from years ago. We occasionally have conflict of interest issues. The understanding of our abilities. High-powered data work. Individualized audiences may know us for one thing but don't know all that we do. The lingering idea of how do we know we're doing any good. How can we prove things are getting better—it's a very difficult thing to do. How do we tease out what part of improvement is us, and what part is the work of others? There aren't a lot of agencies in the market that do what we do—we don't have many competitors. It tends to be non-profit organizations doing the work, so it is dominated by organizations that have been in the business a long time.

5 What's Truly in It for Them

The credible, independent resource for improvement of your health care.

6 True to My Word

Improvement

7 A Matter of Facts

We're the only independent health care quality improvement organization offering expertise, tools and techniques to help you provide the best care to your patients. We have a 30-year history of working and partnering with every major professional health care organization and health care providers across the state. Throughout all these projects, the results were better than where things stood at the beginning of the project. We help providers get ever closer to giving the right care to every person, every time. Our staff is supremely credentialed and experienced—people look to us as the leading guide toward medical quality. We are completely objective in our mission—we aren't "selling" anything. We're completely independent and not affiliated with other organizations that would affect our decision-making. We are a non-profit. We understand Medicare. We understand Medicaid. We understand both the strengths and weaknesses of today's health care system. We are a respected, trusted convener and have a proven record of bringing historic competitors together to improve care and share their successes and wisdom. We also bring a valuable connectivity with other health care quality improvement organizations throughout the nation. We are "locally based, nationally connected." We are ensuring the healthiest lives possible.

8 Cause for Action

Visit our website.

9 Our True Voice

Our voice is credible. Flexible. Business casual. Proactive. A listener. We answer questions well. We're a female voice. More verbal than visual. Intellectual over emotional. Blue, green, gray—quiet, muted colors. Serif font. Oak tree.

10 True to Form

Immediate tools include a new logo, stationery package, proposal cover, website, templates for reports, email newsletter, general newsletter and internal communications.

City Early Childhood Education Program

1 Our True Cause

To improve the quality of early childhood education thereby improving our economic security and quality of life.

2 Why Tell Our Truth?

Proactively communicating with our key audiences is necessary for the achievement of improving the quality of early childhood education (childcare) for all children in our City. Through a positive public information/education campaign, city taxpayers will realize that investing in and improving the quality of early childhood education will in fact improve their quality of life.

3 Tell "Me" the Truth

Taxpayers

4 What's Stopping Us from Telling the Truth

Lack of public awareness of the issue. Mayor's race. Lots of non-profit competition. Organizations like the United Way's efficient social responsibility. Negative image of kids. Funding with schools. The $billion+ deficit. Funding for crime, "rework" and remedial programs. Unions. People numbed by bad news. Backlash to 4-year-old kindergarten—don't like idea of ABC's taught so young. Home-schoolers. Mom stays at home, child left behind. Ability to admit we aren't doing as good a job as we should. Perception that city already is a provider of quality child-care. Perception that this is a problem for only the poor. Perception that this is a minority problem. Looking for positive change in effectiveness of public education. Voters need to see this is their issue.

5 What's Truly in It for Them

Quality early childcare education is an intelligent investment in your economic security.

6 True to My Word

Intelligent

7 A Matter of Facts

Ninety percent of our brain develops by the time we are three. That's the kind of growth that would be the envy of Wall Street. By investing in early childhood education you help to produce an economic boom that lasts a lifetime as it improves the life for the child, but also the community and your quality of life. Get $7 back for every $1 you invest. Economic studies show investing in early childhood education delivers a blue chip rate of return. It leads to more efficient and effective schools. Which leads to a more prepared workforce. Which leads to more productivity. Which leads to increases in lifetime earnings. Not investing would be criminal. Positive emotional and intellectual development leads to greater community responsibility, which leads to a reduced rate of juvenile delinquency and need for prison space. Investing in early childhood education is a no-brainer.

8 Cause for Action

Invest and support quality early childhood education in our city. Visit *www.brightandearly.org* and join the coalition.

9 Our True Voice

This is a message founded upon truths—it is real, authentic—with no reliance on hyperbole or a forced sense of fear. It's a positive message. It is factual. It is also emotional—a message of hope for the future. It is nurturing, secure, with economic benefits underlined with a sense of compassion and humanity. The message isn't loud, but direct and confident. Its colors aren't dark but are captured accurately with bright earth tones. It is a male voice—a sense of earned authority, not macho. The voice can be emotional if appropriate and genuine.

10 True to Form

We are creating a multi-tiered campaign consisting of key media and tactics: Campaign theme/logo, billboards, newspaper ads, website, direct mail, press materials, television, grassroots media, speakers kit/ PowerPoint, cause-marketing sponsorship materials.

Eco-literacy Initiative

1 Our True Cause

To preserve and protect the Great Lakes.

2 Why Tell Our Truth?

To build and motivate a broad constituency to protect biodiversity, telling our story is part of our cause. We are, in fact, an organization where communication is part of our purpose. If we don't communicate, we fail our mission. Specific to our initiative to preserve and protect the Great Lakes, public education is a bedrock element for our success.

3 Tell "Me" the Truth

Lifestylers—they already know and care about the lakes. These are people who seek out the Great Lakes, they have a mental picture, these are not just people who live next to lakes, but they go to the lakes for recreation, relaxation, etc.

4 What's Stopping Us from Telling the Truth

We don't have a product to sell, other than the Great Lakes. Our product becomes a website that links to other organizations (active involvement). Exploitation of the Great Lakes image to sell products. It's not just the ecosystem, but the whole society—diluting the message, redefining the agenda. The Sports Page—defining concerns as scare tactics, and telling people not to worry (i.e., "I eat the fish"). Anti-global warming— some scientist who will say the problems are not related to global warming (i.e., lower lake levels—some people think it is cyclical). Blame to others. Elections drowning out other rhetoric. Myth of infinity and complacency. Beach closings/invasive species/restoration policy—competing campaigns create clutter. Individual environmental messages that are not on the same page (i.e., crisis, alarming campaigns). Tourism, similar messages from tourism boards. Environmental images are used to sell everything. The threat of turning the Great Lakes into a commodity instead of recognizing them as a natural resource. People love the lakes, but think the DNR or EPA are taking care of them—good, well-intentioned people are taking care of things. An absence of "urgency." Daily individual worries, don't ask me to put one more thing on my list—I'm too busy. What difference can I make? Legislators don't see Great Lakes initiatives as a "vote getter." Ecological disasters will take attention away. Competition of each individual lake as opposed to the collective whole. It's not just the lake, it's the whole ecosystem. Perception of the Great Lakes that there's nothing wrong and it is someone else's responsibility. How to take a complex idea and turn it into a clear and compelling message.

5 What's Truly in It for Them

You can turn your concern about your vulnerable Great Lakes into immediate action that can help save your Great Lakes.

6 True to My Word

Your

7 A Matter of Facts

Our thorough understanding of the issues helps us serve as a source for action—action that helps make sure the benefits of the Great Lakes continue—benefits such as fresh air, clean water, places to play, wonderful wildlife and thriving industry. We have the tools, resources and partnerships necessary to translate your action into action that will preserve the Great Lakes for future generations to come while at the same time impacting today's quality of life, the economy and sustainable tourism. We have the ability to be your resource in answering questions and solving problems regarding water quantity, water export, over-consumption concerns, pollution, habitat protection, loss of habitat, invasive species, native biodiversity and poorly planned development concerns. We can help create policy that will prevent unhealthy exports and overuse within the ecosystem.

8 Cause for Action

You can turn your concern about your vulnerable Great Lakes into immediate action that can help save your Great Lakes. Visit the website. Take action.

9 Our True Voice

Our voice is hopeful. Positive. Successful. "Together." Passionate. Visual. Emotional.

10 True to Form

We need several tools to help tell our story. Those tools include: full-page ads in lifestyle magazines; radio; movie screen slides; grocery bags; coastal coasters; posters.

Family Planning Campaign

1 Our True Cause

To make the world a better place for women.

2 Why Tell Our Truth?

As healthcare providers, we work to empower women of reproductive age by ensuring free and confidential access to birth-control services. To fulfill this promise, it is critical that we communicate with women, to connect and let them know our story, which is in fact their story.

3 Tell "Me" the Truth

Women, 17–22 in urban setting, and women, 17–22 in rural setting.

4 What's Stopping Us from Telling the Truth

Lack of money to do promotional work. Perception that birth control is abortion, that condoms don't work. Religious beliefs. Politics. Cultural disconnects. Social norms. "Can't happen in my neighborhood." What they wish for and what they do. Head versus body—facts in "head" are inaccurate. General distrust of birth control. Paperwork. Less attention to health when in economic need. Disenfranchised—health is last issue during survival mode. Don't want to be on government program. The times clinics are open. Clinic access. Transportation. Complicated system, multiple providers. Lack of education about what providers do. Controversial image of family planning (Planned Parenthood). Perception of public services: Low income = poor services. Preference to have personal physician. Pro-lifers. Abstinence movement. Scare tactics. Not being taught "health choices." For-profit clinics. Peers. Partners. Parents. Culture. Media. Taboo topic. Stigma of disease. Limited English proficiency. The economy.

5 What's Truly in It for Them

You can get confidential and free birth control as well as STD testing.

6 True to My Word

Confidential

7 A Matter of Facts

We have a proven history of being confidential. If you don't have a trusted friend look to us as your trusted and informed source as we have built accuracy into our system. We are women and understand women and have a unique passion for women and children. We follow quality control indicators and are trained in family planning and are recognized specialists in women's health and the reproductive system. We are publicly funded family planning specialists and are partners with our clients. We don't judge, lecture or moralize. Our website and phone system are confidential. We provide a safety net not found at general clinics and make access affordable and free when eligible.

8 Cause for Action

You can get confidential and free birth control as well as STD testing. Visit *www.psssst.org* for a clinic near you (phone number when appropriate).

9 Our True Voice

Our voice is upbeat. Caring. Confidential. Confident. Directed at person, intimate. The voice of your "trusted" friend, your "together" friend, your "successful" girlfriend—solid, para-professional. Some sophistication, not naïve. Sexual connotations. Clever. Sense of immediacy, now! Sense of choice, empowerment.

10 True to Form

We need several tools to help tell our story. Those tools include: campaign theme, logo, ads, posters, billboards, wallet cards, movie slides, radio, TV, website, event handouts, clinic displays, family planning clinic communication kits.

Western Environmental Advocacy

1 Our True Cause

To preserve and protect the environment of the Interior West.

2 Why Tell Our Truth?

To raise awareness of the land, water, and energy issues facing the Interior West and our effective, multi-disciplinary approach to resolving them. Our purpose is to preserve and protect the environment of the Interior West through law, policy, advocacy and partnerships. We believe sharing our story and having conversations (marketing) with our audiences is vital to fulfilling our mission. We believe our story is powerful enough to capture the "hearts and minds" of westerners (those who live in the west and those who don't but still are in love with it). We believe by capturing our audience both emotionally and intellectually, we will have the necessary funding and resources to keep our organization and our purpose alive and thriving.

3 Tell "Me" the Truth

A general public/major donor "persona" who is capable of giving $1000.

4 What's Stopping Us from Telling the Truth

Although troublesome to consider our clients and partners as competitors, they are. Shrinking foundation assets leads to cutthroat regional competition. Labels such as "environmentalist." Governments. Defensive versus offensive. Counterintuitive, paradoxical messages that take time to understand. Lack of money. Outside perceptions include: too compartmentalized, driven by funding, organizational "condominium" style. Lack of presence in enough states, lack of perception even among those who know us (including Board members).

5 What's Truly in It for Them

We restore and protect the environment in the Interior West.

6 True to My Word

Protect

7 A Matter of Facts

We are the only environmental organization of our kind committed to this geographic region. We promote solutions to the difficult environmental problems in our region so that we can live here sustainably. We are truly multi-disciplinary in our approach, featuring a winning team of attorneys, advocates and analysts. The scope of our activities allows us to yield analytic and advocacy economies of scale. The success of our Lands Program range from protecting wild landscapes and biodiversity to grazing reforms and defending special public lands from oil and gas development. Our Energy Program's ongoing achievements include the promoting of clean, renewable resources of power, improving air quality and decreasing global warming, increasing efficiencies with the energy we use, forming partnerships, promoting sustainable policies creating green marketing campaigns. Our water program successes include maintaining healthy rivers, protecting endangered species and fragile rivers, restoring resources and habitats, initiating innovative programs such as "Smart Cities, Smart Water," reforming the operation of federal dams and facilities. We form successful, strategic partnerships— over 120 partnerships last year alone. And we host a vibrant, effective volunteer program.

8 Cause for Action

Seek more information about us that results in financial and/or resource support (via website, events, direct contact—depending on situation).

9 Our True Voice

Our voice is pragmatic yet passionate. We are collaborative but can be combative. We are eggheads, thoughtful "wonks." We are persuasive, influential, confident, and know our stuff. We are also hard working, professional and dedicated. We can be arrogant, we can be chameleon-like. Colors that capture our personality would be vibrant, ranging from bright green to purple to cobalt blue. The Red Fox could be our mascot. We are optimistic, but can rely on negative words and images to make our point.

10 True to Form

We will be applying our message to a number of tools: new name, new identity, websites, psa's (radio, billboard, TV, theatre), electronic and print mailers, brochures, exhibits, press kits and releases, templates for talks and proposals, action alerts, op-eds, talking point cards.

National Environmental Advocacy Organization

1 Our True Cause

To protect the nation's environment by making state activist groups successful.

2 Why Tell Our Truth?

People accept state by state that it's important to do something, but they're not accepting that it leads to something important at the national level—we need to be convincing about how the collective state-by-state effort is enormously important to the national environment. We are the voice for state-level activist groups advocating for the environment in the broadest sense. In the environmental movement, the very local or national or international concerns are known, but not the statewide concerns—therefore, it is important for us to get our word out. Marketing will enhance recognition and appreciation of the role we play with key audiences, particularly foundations. There's some educating that needs to be done—it's a big part of the communications effort—people need to understand that it counts in their lives, they need to know where they can do something. We have set a much more ambitious agenda for ourselves, so it is necessary to tell our story at a number of levels: national level, funders, member groups, and other state-level groups who haven't joined us.

3 Tell "Me" the Truth

Funders

4 What's Stopping Us from Telling the Truth

How we see ourselves versus how the funders see us. How to measure our impact (internal and external issue). The real challenge is for outsiders to understand us—to harness us and to justify it to the funders. We may appear as a closed club where others are not entirely welcome and the funders may see that. You see the value because you're in the club—the challenge is how do we open this up to be more effective and open? Disparate groups/our need to define the value of the organization—the way the different member organizations see us and our value can vary significantly—internal cohesion. Difficult to get the media to pay attention to us. Middle ground between national and local, compounded by the limited amount of money given to the entire environmental quadrant, total of philanthropic pie is between 2 to 3 percent, majority of this is going to buy land (Nature Conservancy/Land Trusts). Many components to give money to in the environmental movement: education, advocacy, building capacity in the trade. Some people are "green-washing," but others really don't get it. Our protection is over the long haul—we're protecting—it's much harder because we're trying to change behavior. When you can make a compelling case it is very rewarding. There are groups that understand that what we do is fundamentally political, and very difficult. Unless we can enhance the fortitude and provide more tools for these organizations, we're not going to make a difference. We need to get people to listen long enough. We need to add things up and connect things to the national level. Politicians are thinking in term lengths—whereas we're thinking of generations/ecosystems. Psychological barrier—getting organizations (whose directors have their own jobs/lives to lead) to engage with us is difficult. The economy. Our name.

5 **What's Truly in It for Them**

We provide 50 ways to protect America's environment.

6 **True to My Word**

50

7 **A Matter of Facts**

We are a nationwide network of over 50 independent, non-profit, public interest, multi-issue environmental advocacy organizations that work to affect strong state environmental protection policies. From fighting factory farms and increasing penalty amounts to multi-media campaigns on mercury to helping state organizations expand from 150,000 members to 400,000—we get things done. This year alone, several thousand bills will be introduced in state legislatures that could impact the quality of our water, air, wildlife habitat, and public health. Effective state environmental protection policies will only be achieved in these increasingly burdened state governments with the efforts of increasingly vigilant state environmental advocacy movements. We are the catalyst and champion of these state advocacy movements. We work with members and allies to identify particular issues of concern, facilitate strategy meetings to bring together advocates working on similar issues, analyze model state policies, programs and strategies and generally act as a clearinghouse for information. We provide organizational capacity building opportunities, facilitate strategy exchange on select policy and organizational issues among member groups, and coordinate multi-state environmental issue campaigns in which member groups may participate. We can actually show you 50 ways we have helped protect America's environment.

8 **Cause for Action**

Invest in America's environment, write a check.

9 **Our True Voice**

Our voice gives clarity on what the problems are. An adult woman—in the sense of bearing the next generation. Young enough to still be optimistic, but old enough to have a perspective on the world. Strong. Articulate. Inquisitive. Idealism and belief in a better world. Our language needs to be more straightforward, eighth grade reading level, not at a high level. We don't lecture. We have a breadth of interests. In charge. Long-term. Athletic, enjoys the environment. Has a child or children. Listens first, but not afraid to talk—engages in conversation. Visual color scheme: earth tones. Wool socks, comfortable shoes, fleece, what's most comfortable. Simple, smart. Supports Fair Trade. Not Birkenstocks and dreadlocks. Transportation: bike, public transportation, owns a Prius (she drives, but would feel guilty about it). Serious and silly at the same time. Sans serif font. Straightforward. Wildflower. Pet: larger-sized mutt from the humane society.

10 True to Form

We will need talking points (the 50 ways we protect the American environment), folders, presentation materials, overall brochure, e-alerts, website, vision document, monthly activist reports/update, testimonials and a "suite" of communication materials.

Child Advocacy Organization

1 Our True Cause

To relentlessly provide hope and opportunity for every child in the state.

2 Why Tell Our Truth?

We have a compelling story. We need to tell our story in order to obtain the funds to do the work that needs to be done. We can't do this by ourselves, we need groundswell. We need to show connections. We need to change policy and get people to vote differently—this requires education, which means we need to be telling our story when and wherever possible. We are trying to engage the public in what leads to a change in public will. We need to talk about the issues, show the impact, and reveal the value of the organization. To echo our cause, we must be relentless and focused in our communications and make the most of all communications opportunities.

3 Tell "Me" the Truth

Wealthy, influential people.

4 What's Stopping Us from Telling the Truth

We have some competition, economic barriers and psychological obstacles that serve as "bumps in the road" as we move forward. Those bumps include: The state budget. The National budget. Our budget. The current U.S. President/Administration. The geography of our state. A sense that the state feels like two states, a "schizophrenic state." Direct service providers. The advocacy line item is typically marked off the list during tough times. Taking us for granted. The public's value of short-term gratification versus commitment to the long haul. Lots of other non-profits asking the same people. Competing with the value proposition of arts and environmental issues and organizations. The "concrete-ness" of competition, for example, the ballet. We have created our own advocacy competition. The child health arena. The western value of independence versus our championing of community. A sea of not-for-profits emerging from a "start something new" mentality. Non-profit territorialism. We could spread ourselves too thin. Our innate competitiveness can be our own worst enemy.

5 What's Truly in It for Them

You can create hope and opportunity in our state one million kids at a time.

6 True to My Word

Million

7 A Matter of Facts

For over 20 years, we've been the leading force behind initiatives and policies that protect and provide for our children. We deliver a strong financial ROI and a strong emotional ROI. We are completely accountable, innovative and strategic. We are entrepreneurial and capitalize on opportunities. We are not bureaucratic or slow. We have no agenda except providing hope and opportunity for our kids. We leverage the private dollars we raise to ensure that public funds are used effectively to support children's health, education and development. For every $1 we spend on advocacy, $10 of public money is channeled to direct service programs for children. The effects of our work are seen every day when low-income children receive health and dental care, when at-risk youth escape from the streets into structured, caring community centers and when quality schools ensure that every child has an education that opens the doors to future success. We effectively lobby at all governmental and legislative levels and propose policy and ballot initiatives. We provide effective grassroots assistance and programmatic management. We are the experts. We are setting the state's agenda on children. We provide you with the real opportunity to help a million kids.

8 Cause for Action

We want our primary audience to write at least a $1,000 check. We also want our supporters to get and stay involved.

9 Our True Voice

We definitely have a personality and certain distinct character traits. We are relentless, fearless and determined. We are strategic. We are flexible in the savvy sense of the word. We are gifted in building coalitions. We reflect the new type of corporate environment—dynamic, trustful, fast. We are optimistic. We challenge. We're bold. If we have a color, it would be a bold purple. We are more sans serif than serif if we were a typeface. If we were a landmark in the West, it would be Independence Pass. We enjoy language and are more verbal than visual. We can be a little academic. Although we tend to have a female voice, we are not very "ladylike." We can be egocentric and self-righteous. We embrace risk. Love the numbers. Have no problem hanging out with millionaires, the ambitious and the elite. We emit authority, command and expertise. We are getting more playful and funders think we are "fun." We are connected to our "million" word and all the meanings it conveys. If our organization has a face, it would be our Director's. We should consider our current logo/identity and how it works with this personality as well as the other strategic insights found in this document.

10 True to Form

We need several key communication tools. We should also consider investing in these tools so that many of them don't need to be reinvented for the 20th Anniversary. Particularly, we need: written materials for 20th anniversary committee, a stand-alone piece, a short, crisp version of talking points, updated website, tagline, mission statement, library of images, photos and icons, templates (including email) and logo update, templates and fundraising materials.

Convention & Visitors Bureau

1 Our True Cause

To make sure as many people as possible experience the fact that we meet both their emotional and intellectual needs.

2 Why Tell Our Truth?

To make sure as many people as possible experience the fact that we meet both their emotional and intellectual needs, we need to increase optimum levels of visitor traffic. To do this we need to connect with as many potential visitors as possible. The results of this connection will sustain and enhance the quality of life here, help local business stay healthy and grow and provide a great way for all kinds of ideas and perspectives to be exchanged and shared.

3 Tell "Me" the Truth

Meeting planners in national associations, particularly engineering, environmental, agri-business, biomedical/medical.

4 What's Stopping Us from Telling the Truth

Other cities/destinations: Portland for environmental. Pittsburgh for engineering. Kansas City and Louisville for agri-business. State Fair Park. Large convention centers bordering our region. First tier destinations. Other new facilities. Air service—people think we're hard to get to—perception of transportation. One less connection in major city. Slightly more expensive to get here. Lack of support in the community from civic leaders. Citizens and elected officials not sure they want more business here. Self-satisfied people—we've got it nice here, why share it? Perception that we're too small. Large meeting facilities are relatively new on the scene. Lack of large first-class hotels/guest rooms. Weather! Incentive monies (cash and in-kind incentives)—can't compete with larger markets. Bureau funding—lack of marketing resources to get the word out. Target of peak 300 room nights—planners are used to meeting in large convention hotels—all under one roof. Necessity here to use several facilities. We may be too close to other big metro areas. May be more expensive than a convention hotel because of multiple facilities. Hotel rates/facility fees: economic conditions are driving hotel and facility rates down in many destinations creating a "buyer's market," rendering our "affordability" premise less palatable. There may be a longer decision-making process. Harder for a smaller-sized market—not the sense of urgency as with a large convention destination. Price/value— not a good area we can compete in. Disparity between perception and reality. We could become too popular for our market—some local groups may become tired from helping to organize too many meetings here; attendees may feel they are coming here too often. Two biggest things in our way: lack of awareness and perception of being too small.

5 What's Truly in It for Them

We meet both your intellectual and emotional needs.

6 True to My Word

Both

7 A Matter of Facts

Our location makes sense geographically—it's centrally located. Transportation is not a problem—we are easy to get to. Great value in a classic setting. We rate extremely high in attendance and satisfaction. We have survey results rating us high in the areas of destination reputation, friendliness, safety, CVB service, restaurants, shopping and attendee popularity when compared to other destinations. Research shows that 54 percent of meeting professions reported significant attendance increases for their convention compared to their previous conventions in other destinations. You'll be in a safer environment (over larger destinations). It's more affordable (over larger destinations)—we have the versatility to host groups from 10 to 10,000. Access to internationally renowned university. We're known among the academic and scientific communities to be one of the most attractive and interesting cities. We'll save you time. We provide you with facility and hotel proposals that accommodate your needs. We do all the legwork.

We believe in what we sell as a destination because we live it and enjoy being here. Madison is beautiful and real—it's authentic. No other city has as many "rankings" as Madison. We have hosted signature events in your industry. You will not be disappointed by coming here.

8 Cause for Action

Go to our trade show booth and seek us out. Call (phone number) or visit our website at www.*visitmadison.com*

9 Our True Voice

Our voice is smart, yet funny. People-oriented. Casual but vibrant. Approachable. Confident. We have a female voice. Not aggressive, but assertive. Mildly aloof. We're like chocolate, but even better.

10 True to Form

We are creating a business-to-business campaign that will require a campaign theme, series of segmented print ads, direct mailers, trade show booth, website application, public relations, press materials, editorial submissions.

International Fair Trader

1 Our True Cause

To alleviate poverty.

2 Why Tell Our Truth?

Our story and cause is the value added piece to our product—people will buy a product with a cause. We need to create an environment in which our producers will be able to sell their products. This is a marketing company and a marketing company inherently must market itself. We couldn't function without telling our story effectively.

3 Tell "Me" the Truth

The *Cultural Creative* group concerned about dealing with meaningful organizations; people we already have but lower the age to 25 to 50.

4 What's Stopping Us from Telling the Truth

In the past we were unique because our products came from all over the world—the difference now is that we do have competition. There are like products out there. It's difficult to get our message out. We can't compete with what customers see when they walk into a store. We're constantly checking other stores for the products they are offering. Although we are striving to develop a unique product line, we may offer products similar to those available elsewhere to assist our producer partners to generate income. We have a customer base that prefers to buy from us, and for which uniqueness is an issue. Coming soon—competition in message. Eziba (funding from AOL) and Novica (related to *National Geographic*). It's a tough business. Gift market has been in a huge downturn. People aren't buying as much as they used to. Not making purchases of Christmas items (or Easter or Halloween). Shoppers are buying more utilitarian-type items. There was a big gift business before, but now trying to have products that are more useful—movement from gift to real use. Extremely difficult business market. Other businesses are looking for cool products that have already been imported to the U.S. Good guy/bad guy thing isn't good to get into. Psychological obstacles: People think of fair trade as inexpensive. We have had a problem of under pricing our products with low price points. Haven't found an effective way to tell our story broadly—people don't understand who we are and what we do. We need to differentiate ourselves from everything else that's out there. When large corporations co-opt the fair trade message when less than 1 percent of their products are fair trade—they have amazing success in reaching and capturing a younger customer.

5 What's Truly in It for Them

We provide the opportunity to enjoy products that enrich your life and change the world.

6 True to My Word

Opportunity

7 A Matter of Facts

One of the first alternative trade organizations in the world, we've been around for 54 years and we have real life stories to show how lives have been changed. We change the values people bring to their trading activities and we do this with minimal expense—cost/benefit ratio of what we do is very high. Our products are very appealing. We offer a 30-day money back guarantee and excellent customer service. We reinvest any profits in our program and our producer partners. We partner with more than 85 community-based groups in 35 developing nations, all committed to eliminating poverty through fair trade. We advance as much as 50 percent of the final product price to artisans to purchase raw materials and pay producer partners fair prices within the context of their local economy. We provide thousands of artisans and family members with supplemental or total annual income. We are a founding member of IFAT (and embrace the IFAT Code of Practice, which defines the fundamental values and principles behind alternative trade) and FTF (Fair Trade Federation of North America) and Green Business. We invest in people, products and relationships. We accomplish a lot with a limited amount of resources.

8 Cause for Action

Ultimately, connect with our mission and our products via website, toll-free fax, toll-free phone, mail, catalog, and store.

9 Our True Voice

Our voice is less shy and reserved than in the past but not bold. Our voice is personal and relationship-oriented. We are active, energetic and responsible. Our voice is female. We are honest, caring and authentic but not mushy or romantic. We're global in our understanding of diversity and how people connect in the world. We're down to earth but worldly in global issues. We're down to earth yet sophisticated. We are rich with history and vision. We have a heritage yet we are contemporary. We're simple and optimistic. We look for and offer opportunity. We work hard to do what we can do well. We're pragmatic but not pretentious. We take concrete actions. We're diverse. We like doing business and are serious about what we do. We're pleasant as opposed to fun. We're not cute or funky. We're not formal or cosmopolitan. We're smart and focused. We're no-nonsense. We're not red!

10 True to Form

Naming first, then integrate into all other components—from catalogue to website to PowerPoint and product labels.

Economic Development Corporation

1 Our True Cause

To create the context for courageous business conversations.

2 Why Tell Our Truth?

Our cause and communicating our cause go hand-in-hand. If we are to create the context for courageous business conversations, we need to have courageous conversations with our audiences. They need to know we are here to answer this need and our leadership role in doing so. If we don't get the word out about our cause, we will not fulfill it.

3 Tell "Me" the Truth

Business leader.

4 What's Stopping Us from Telling the Truth

Status quo. Fear of change. Fear of collaboration. Lack of understanding of new business model. Organization size and resources.

5 What's Truly in It for Them

We create the context for finding business solutions together through courageous business conversation.

6 True to My Word

Conversation

7 A Matter of Facts

Nowhere else can you get the knowledge we provide. We help create real business conversations. We are truly objective facilitators of significant dialogues, conversations, meetings. We help businesses find solutions together. We honor and shepherd the evolution of solutions. We address critical issues and issues of current and critical interest. We are an accessible reservoir of ideas. We produce real intellectual capital. We help establish a positive legacy for businesses. We translate, interpret, connect and strengthen. We scale and dismantle walls. We showcase economic engines. We help business realize they are part of something larger and that no one of us is the answer. We are the "lifeline over the silos." We are the only organization looking at regional opportunities. We are the touchstone for rewarding business relationships and conversations because we have truly valuable information to impart. We are a "servant leader" and make life easier for business. We are agents of change for the better. We go where no one has been before and actually look forward to going there. The journey is always good for business.

8 Cause for Action

We want our audience to become part of the conversation. To learn more about us and inquire about how they can participate in the conversations.

9 Our True Voice

Our voice is refreshing and confident. Our voice listens. It is objective, unbiased and inclusive. Our voice is very much like our primary audience. It, too, honors tolerance and celebrates differences of ideas. Our voice respects all ethnicities, ages and structures. Our voice believes people are the key to future economic development. Our voice sees the big picture but has a regional accent. Our voice is one of "facilitator with authority" a "context creator with a destination." Our voice is passionate about business. Our voice has local roots and cares about the community. Our voice is punctuated by social responsibility.

10 True to Form

To begin, we will need presentation materials for talks and exhibits, brochure, pledge cards, web application, direct mail, dialogue captures and an integrated advertising effort.

Master of Management in Hospitality Program

1 Our True Cause

To create a global community of hospitality leaders who change the world.

2 Why Tell Our Truth?

The story has to be told. There is no choice! Specifically, we must tell our story for two reasons: so people understand and so people get excited and want to learn more. The industry doesn't know what the degree is exactly. Grads use the term MBA, when it's not an MBA and we don't need to use MBA. We must communicate that an MMH is different from an MBA. Authenticity and honesty with communications is needed. We need to communicate what's different, what's the same. Three things need additional explanation: why global; how can you do in one year what we did in two years; and career tracks.

3 Tell "Me" the Truth

Prospective students

4 What's Stopping Us from Telling the Truth

Everything from lack of program understanding to other schools to resources to ourselves.

5 What's Truly in It for Them

Create a global community of hospitality leaders who change the world.

6 True to My Word

Community

7 A Matter of Facts

This Master of Management in Hospitality (MMH) program is a graduate business degree unlike any other. The program's driving purpose is to create a global community of hospitality leaders who change the world. Offered by the world's number one hospitality school, the MHH experience is intense, innovative and inspiring and sought by industry professionals, recent graduates and career changers who have an unstoppable passion for hospitality and performance. The MMH is truly international with program options at both our New York and Singapore campuses. This one delivers worldwide networking opportunities, hands-on understanding of global business practice and expertise in today's fastest growing hospitality markets. Our strategic, marketable career-tracks merge passion for the field with the skill, know-how and insight necessary to immediately solve problems and impact business. The intensive three-semester, one year, AACSB-accredited program delivers profound returns on investment. MMH graduates are entrepreneurs, restaurateurs, developers, analysts and consultants, corporate directors and managers of hotels, resorts and spas. The world-renowned faculty lead the learning experience and serve as a resource for insights on cutting-edge developments in the field and connections with key industry leaders. An alumni network that spans the globe and continuous interaction with executives also generate outstanding career opportunities.

8 Cause for Action

Prospective students: apply/enroll.
Career Track Companies: Hire our graduates. Get involved in program. Send us and support recruits.

9 Our True Voice

Our voice is caring, inclusive. Exciting, communal. Joyful, passionate. Bright colors, contemporary. Gender: fluid, mix of male and female voices, not strongly male or female. Not a tree, but a forest: not a flower, but a wildflower garden.

10 True to Form

We will integrate our strategy into various tools, beginning with a campaign theme and identity (applicable to both student/industry audiences), student and industry talking points, case studies/testimonials, student and industry brochures, ads, print and emails, web applications and electronic and print templates.

Market Research Company

1 Our True Cause

Creating better places to live and work.

2 Why Tell Our Truth?

Speaking is a large part of our communications effort and revenue. If we don't tell our story, there will be inhumane places for people to work—if cities don't attract young talent, older people won't pass an increase in taxes for education, people/businesses won't want to move into the area—it's a downward spiral. From the perspective of an economist, a compelling piece of this story is that any city that's interested in their tax base needs to hear our message because there are more Baby Boomers than Gen Xers. We always lead with stories. People are most captivated by stories. People may forget your talking point but they'll remember the story. Emotionally is how people internalize the essence of our cause.

3 Tell "Me" the Truth

Young-minded people who can effect positive change in their communities.

4 What's Stopping Us from Telling the Truth

Gurus such as Richard Florida—maybe/maybe not (he creates awareness and we come in with methodology). We are offering a very unique service, and Richard Florida validates our work because he is more theory and we're more action. We don't get the sense that we have competition—people are excited to find out that what Rich Florida is talking about is actionable. The only ones doing similar work are those promoting "people first, profits second" attitude. Within corporate America, people bat around names of huge consulting companies. The huge companies charge so much, and we can provide much more "juice for the squeeze." Reputational capital—sometimes has to do with size, ability to work with scale. Our reputational capital has to be around our uniqueness.

5 What's Truly in It for Them

You will engage the next generation.

6 True to My Word

Engage

7 A Matter of Facts

We are the experts—since 1997 we've interviewed over 7,000 GenXers and Young Professionals. Nobody knows more about the next generation than us. No one knows more about what young talent wants, dreams and needs than us. Faced with more job options and greater mobility than previous generations, young talent identify more strongly with their communities than their companies. Our Talent Capital report is a starting point for community self-assessment. We can help assess a community's "coolness," build an innovative talent campaign, and show communities where to recruit. We will help you determine who the right talent is. We help you find focus. We create discussions that really engage people at a higher level and start new thinking. We conduct web-based surveys and focus groups—we go directly to the talent. We spend time on the ground with one-on-one interviews in coffee shops with young talent to find out what people really value. Then, we'll follow them home and see if they live what they say. Combine the framework and measurement tools we've developed with our research, expertise and knowledge and we are the proven access point for talent engagement.

8 Cause for Action

Engage us.

9 Our True Voice

We are bold, ourselves, cool, classy. Brave. Pioneers. Truth-tellers. Female-voice (inclusive, values-driven, innovative). Listener (focus group/research). Visual. Sherbet colors with gray (lime green, bright yellow). Suit is classy, accessories are trendy. We tell good stories/humorous/playful/having a sense of fun. Casual. We ride a bike or drive a bright-colored convertible. We have a garden with bright, colorful, different flowers. Lush green. Free-range. A little wild. Inclusion—fountain, flowers, stone, etc. A little unusual—a surprise, something someone could learn from, or ask, "Why did you choose to put that there?"

10 True to Form

We will need an updated website, brochure, postcards/direct mailer, newsletter, email flashes, press-kit, proposal templates, PowerPoint templates, ads possibly.

Medical Insurance Company

1 Our True Cause

To help eliminate fear from the practice of medicine.

2 Why Tell Our Truth?

To help eliminate fear from the practice of medicine. It is important to tell our value story—that when you need us we are here. We want to share quantifiable information. We want to have differentiated ourselves in a soft market. We want to be sure to chisel a position others may try but can't occupy. We need to show how we walk the talk and how we are not a commodity. Communications and marketing will help us achieve these objectives.

3 Tell "Me" the Truth

Physician policyholders.

4 What's Stopping Us from Telling the Truth

Other insurance companies. Plaintiff attorneys. Self-insurance. Risk retention. Alternative risk transfer programs. Going bare (not buying insurance). Territories. Regulators. Legislators. Our size. Bad media. Reinsurers. Non-agents. Some shareholders. Ourselves.

5 What's Truly in It for Them

We practice insurance courageously so you can practice courageous medicine.

6 True to My Word

Courageous

7 A Matter of Facts

We do what's right, not what's expedient. Because we are physician-owned and controlled, there is no conflict of interest between customers' needs, board expectations, and responsible use of capital. There was pressure to lower prices during price wars and not do the right thing. We held our ground. We bring stability to medical professional liability insurance. This is our core business and we have developed extensive expertise by concentrating solely on this market. We have had an AM Best A- (Excellent) rating for many years. We defend the hell out of our policyholders. We partner with the very best counsel, closing roughly 90 percent of our claims without indemnity payment. We take the long view instead of going for short-term profit. We engage with our customers and they actively participate in the reduction of risk. We are a thoughtful company at all points whether it's the initial pricing, the constellation of services offered, the risk management, etc. We don't believe insurance is a commodity product. We're always looking to change and grow and be a better company whether it's personnel or changes to infrastructure. This company attracts people who are striving for excellence.

8 Cause for Action

Pass the word. We want every policyholder to recommend us. For more information call your agent or us at (phone number) or visit (website).

9 Our True Voice

We are reliable and accountable. We are financially strong. We are David fighting Goliath. We are Braveheart. We speak softly and carry a big stick. We are a family, caring about employees and our community. We sympathize when competitors fail. Strong ethics ensure we do the right thing—we agonize over doing the right thing. We're not a "black and white" organization. We're not "all things to all people." We're intelligent and selective. We strive for excellence. We are foxhole buddies with physicians. We are levelers of the playing field—defenders of physicians' reputations. We are indignant when good physicians are treated badly.

We are honest—we don't hide the truth from our policyholders. We are team players. We are respectful of our customers. We are ingenious and creative. We are entrepreneurial and non-traditional. We are nimble, flexible and collaborative. We're confident and thoughtful. We have high expectations of ourselves and our policyholders. We're energetic and enthusiastic, optimistic and committed. We're not stagnant, always striving to be better—we're never satisfied. We're engaging and passionate. There is a sense of exclusivity with us. We're stable, but more importantly we are fearless. We're courageous.

10 True to Form

We will need both internal and external communication materials. External tools will include theme, print campaign, website, direct mail, proposal formats, report formats, press releases, presentation tools, business segment materials, and PowerPoint templates.

Private School

1 Our True Cause

To create a school where children love to come learn and find joy in learning.

2 Why Tell Our Truth?

We're here to create a school where children "Love To Come To School To Learn." For us to fulfill our purpose and support our cause, it is necessary for us to tell our story. Raising awareness of who we are and what we do is vital to both recruitment and retention. Our audiences need to know we exist, that our "alternative" is real, accessible and of immense value. Telling our story is also necessary for overcoming myths, inspiring other schools, combating apathy and making connections to the children who truly do belong in our school.

3 Tell "Me" the Truth

Parents seeking alternatives.

4 What's Stopping Us from Telling the Truth

What people say—we're not academic. Perception of having no structure. Perception of not being the real world. Our kids won't be able to adjust. The economy. The public school system. Parochial schools. Other alternative or private schools. Home schooling. The political system. Power of the teacher's union. The "lefty politically correct" mindset. We're elitist. Our tuition is self-limiting. Perception our size is too small. Our school start is later than most schools. We're not appropriate for every family. The "test" world is results driven. Our scholarships are not sufficient. We haven't been able to express our success without data. Limits to resources such as a gym and athletics. Our facility is old. We are disability noncompliant. We share our building. Not much parking. The need to provide "insurance" that your child will be okay here. The worry that children won't be prepared by going here.

5 What's Truly in It for Them

Learning is joyful here and joyful learners learn more.

6 True to My Word

Joyful

7 A Matter of Facts

We inspire a love of learning—for life. This is a vibrant, caring, safe, enhancing and empowering experience. This is an intellectual, emotional, physical and aesthetic experience. Here, children are truly a part of their education. We respect self-endeavors, childhood and honor the process of growing and learning. This place appreciates differences. We are child-driven, not teacher driven. We don't put our stamp on students. We are progressive and take a constructivist rather than instructivist approach. We are an alternative for alternative family lifestyles. We help children find their place in the world. This is not a "testing" or "grade" environment. We build children's confidence. We are not competitive. We honor the "social I.Q." Everything doesn't have to be "equal" here. We believe it's not what we teach, it's how we teach. Here, it's not a product, it's a process. Likewise, we focus on how to learn. We make information relevant. Our children are inspired to make a positive difference in the world. There are reams of studies that validate the tools we use and the philosophy we embrace. We have over 30 years of experience that makes this all happen! This is a joyful place.

8 Cause for Action

When our audiences hear our message, we would like them to call or email to make an appointment for a visit to the school.

9 Our True Voice

First and foremost, our voice is joyful. It is also vibrant and active. Our voice is credible, confident and rich with authority. Our energy is active. We are a "color outside the lines" personality. We are kind, warm, and friendly. We question. We are reassuring. We have the experience. We are trusted. Our voice is male. There could be a bit of Santa Claus cheer and joy in our voice. If you were to visualize our voice, taking a look at the current photography of our students, teachers, staff and environment would do the trick—it says it all.

10 True to Form

All that we do will be determined by our budget realities, but everything we do should embrace our "joyful, love to learn" positioning. This will call for a recasting of information kits, website, open house ads/flyers/posters. The tools we create should address both enrollment and retention. In terms of an advertising campaign, messages should be developed that can appear in neighborhood newsletters, local papers, perhaps publications like the city magazine and the arts and culture review. It is suggested that the campaign begin by introducing the cause and new theme/positioning in order to carve out an overall image in the market. Then present a series of ads addressing key topics, testimonials, events, etc. We should also consider events, sponsorships, fundraising, educational, learning and community activities that build on our "joyful" and "love to learn" positioning. Media options such as television, radio and outdoor should be considered if media sponsors/partners are engaged to offset the time/space costs.

International Photography Project

1 Our True Cause

To heal divisiveness through individual action.

2 Why Tell Our Truth?

These pictures are worth 10,000 words and they are a very powerful communications force. It would be remiss for us not to utilize these images for the purposes of healing divisiveness. It is the right thing to do and the only real thing to do based on our cause and the resources we have on hand to achieve it. From a practical standpoint, it is imperative we spread the word (and pictures) about who and what we are in order to forge necessary partnerships and alliances. Without telling our story, these partnerships won't occur. And without these partnerships, our initiative will not achieve the tipping point quality it deserves.

3 Tell "Me" the Truth

Organizations/adults directly involved with children and concerned about diversity.

4 What's Stopping Us from Telling the Truth

Racism. Hatred. Intolerance. Climate of fear. Ignorance. Other organizations screaming for help. Political climate. Media climate. Disenfranchisement of children. Funding and resources. Clear understanding of our project.

5 What's Truly in It for Them

This project connects us all and heals the world's divisions with pictures of our humanity.

6 True to My Word

Heals

7 A Matter of Facts

Our 25,000 photographs celebrate childhood around the world and confirm a universal truth: we are all connected. The photographs capture moments ranging from losing our first tooth, taking our first step, making our first friend, but also capture the fact that we are members of a single global family. Without preaching or proselytizing, they instantly communicate the fact that our joy and pride are identical, regardless of our nationality, ethnicity or religion. We capture these universal landmarks of childhood on every continent and compile them into an arresting family of products that communicate our essential message: look, those children are just like me. Right now our words and images are making a difference in airports, libraries, museums and schools around the world and our book (featuring such authors as J. K. Rowling and Walter Cronkite) is being read by adults and children all over the world. We provide practical tools for parents, educators, and opinion formers to help them foster goodhearted children, free of prejudice, intolerance and hatred, and to take personal action to reduce prejudice, intolerance, and hatred in the next three years. If you can picture world peace, partnering with us is an absolute. This is where the real healing begins.

8 Cause for Action

Engage Milestones, end hatred, experience *www.milestonesproject.com*

9 Our True Voice

Milestones is the universal voice of children. We dress in the universal cloth of children. Although the colors on the website are purple and orange, our true colors are the colors of humanity—the colors of our skins, our eyes—and the colors of art and creativity, the color wheel of humanity. When we were to enter a board meeting or dinner party, we would be the person who laughs from the heart, who is curious about everything and everybody, who empathizes with everyone because we, too, have experienced both the pain and joy you experience. We are the person everyone knows they are, may have forgotten they are and because of this moment of interaction, realize they can be. We are dressed in bright, bold colors that attract rather than repel. Our voice is female, nurturing and non-judgmental. We are fearless which inspires the timid to be bold. We are humble which inspires the proud to be compassionate. We aren't a saint; in fact, it's our imperfections that are our most telling characteristic. But it is our embrace of our imperfections that makes others want to be around us. We make people feel safe to be who they truly are. We are the person in the board meeting who speaks their mind from their heart and becomes the natural leader without title. We are the person at the party who everyone wants to leave with and get a cup of coffee and even maybe some ice cream. We are more visual than verbal. We hug a lot because we need to in order to survive.

10   True to Form

Tools are many and include new product applications/tie-ins (puzzles, games, growth charts, etc), talking points, website update, public relations, cause-marketing prospectus, newsletter, DVD, documentary, movie, PBS special, brochure, targeted ads, ambassador kit, events, book package, Google links, grandparents extension/book.

Seeing Is Believing

So, how does your Mission in a Message look and feel? What will be the effect of it?

I hope these cause studies help you shape your final Mission in a Message. Again, I encourage you to go to *www.goodforbusiness.com/book* to see how the briefs become reality in the marketplace. This site reveals all kinds of creative solutions for all kinds of businesses who have embraced the cause-based approach to telling their story. New names, logos, brochures, ads, direct mail, outdoor, packaging, posters, alternative media, websites, and broadcast media are all featured. We know you will find it quite helpful to see these creative translations of communication plans. For us at Good For Business, developing these cause-based messages on behalf of these businesses has and continues to be the most rewarding work we have the honor of creating. You can count on the same kind of gratification when you implement your Mission in a Message as you discover WHY communications make all the difference.

Index

About the Author

JIM ARMSTRONG is founder and creative director of Good For Business, a communications company dedicated to helping clients capture and communicate their cause. Jim believes businesses and organizations aren't just brands, but causes that move hearts, minds and markets. This value proposition results in creating purpose-led communications from which everyone can profit.

In his 25-year career, Jim has helped market everything from safe sex and safe deposit boxes to light pizza and lighting for Broadway to banking in your pajamas and investing in third world countries. He's developed campaigns ranging from AIDS Awareness (on display in the Smithsonian) to World Hunger. Jim has created socially responsible messages in sectors ranging from the environment and energy to education and economic development. His clients around the world include leadership institutes in New Zealand and corporations in the United Kingdom as well as universities in New York.

Prior to founding Good For Business, Jim served as partner and creative director for the nation's leading integrated brand development firm and president and creative director of Armstrong Creative for twelve years. Jim's work has been recognized by the Art Directors Club of New York, *Communication Arts, Print,* and other international peer organizations. He has received more than 500 awards for creativity.

Jim graduated Phi Beta Kappa and has an M.A. in poetry. Through his CorPoet Wordshops, Jim has taught organizations how to explore, find, and validate their core values and beliefs through artistic, poetic expression.

He and his wife Kathy, an artist, have three children, Emily, Megan, and Michael.